The Writer's Guide to

CONQUERING the MAGAZINE MARKET

The Writer's Guide to
CONQUERING
the MAGAZINE
MARKET

CONNIE EMERSON

Cincinnati, Ohio

About the Author

Connie Emerson has sold hundreds of articles to a wide selection of magazines, among them *Travel & Leisure, Antiques Monthly, McCall's, California Business Life* and many others. With the techniques found in *The Writer's Guide to Conquering the Magazine Market*, her sales have consistently outnumbered her rejection slips by more than twenty to one. She and her husband live in Nevada.

The Writer's Guide to Conquering the Magazine Market. Copyright © 1991 by Connie Emerson. Printed and bound in the United States of America. All rights reserved. No part of this book may be reproduced in any form or by any electronic or mechanical means including information storage and retrieval systems without permission in writing from the publisher, except by a reviewer, who may quote brief passages in a review. Published by Writer's Digest Books, an imprint of F&W Publications, Inc., 1507 Dana Avenue, Cincinnati, Ohio 45207. First edition.

95 94 93 92 91   5 4 3 2 1

Library of Congress Cataloging in Publication Data

Emerson, Connie
    The writer's guide to conquering the magazine market / Connie Emerson. — 1st ed.
        p.   cm.
    Includes index.
    ISBN 0-89879-484-6
    1. Authorship—Marketing. 2. Authorship—Handbooks, manuals, etc.
PN161.E5   1991
808'.02 — dc20   91-19590
                                                                        CIP

This book is dedicated to my son,
George Toring Emerson

Contents

Chapter Four
LOOKING AT THE PICTURES 43

Your chances of a sale to many markets are boosted if you can supply photos, too. Study the style and format of a magazine's pictures and adapt the techniques of the pros to keep from shooting yourself — and your hot article ideas — in the foot. Learn how to get great pictures even if you don't own a camera!

Excellent photographs frequently sell an editor on a mediocre story because it's simpler to improve words than pictures. It follows, therefore, that if you are able to include excellent photos with an excellent story, the combination is all but irresistible!

Chapter Five
YOUR STYLE IS MY STYLE 57

What's best — hard-hitting or folksy? Breezy or formal? Lots of direct quotes or paraphrase and overview? It depends on the publication. Learn how to make your writing fit in and give it added punch and appeal, so all editors will know you're *their* kind of writer.

You may have your subject matter down cold. Your grammar and spelling may be above reproach; your title, terrific; your manuscript, unsmudged. The idea may fit its intended publication like a wetsuit. But if you haven't written that article to the editor's stylistic appetites, be doubly sure there's enough postage on that SASE.

Chapter Six
THE NAME GAME 73

An article by the wrong name may not sell. To create interest-grabbing headlines, study the titles to make sure your query or article gets a second look.

If you can devise a just-right title at the time you're querying, your chances of a sale escalate. Upon first glance at your custom-designed title, the editor will see you're on his frequency, and that's the best of all editor-writer beginnings.

Chapter One

Sizing Up Your Chances

*Luck is what happens when
preparation meets opportunity.*

Jack Valenti, *Reader's Digest*

*E*very year millions of tourists visit my city of Reno, Nevada, trying to beat the odds. Precious few do. Each year thousands of would-be article writers try to beat the odds, too. Though they've a better chance than the gambler trying to line up all sevens on a four-reel slot machine (one in 160,000, incidentally), most of them also will be disappointed. The fact is, in the editorial offices of magazines they're most likely to send their hard-written work to, the competition rivals that of trying to find a free parking spot within six blocks of the Super Bowl.

At *Los Angeles Magazine*, from approximately one hundred manuscripts and queries received each month, only one article that's queried about gets a go-ahead on speculation, and staff members can't think of one unsolicited manuscript that has ever been purchased.

The situation is slightly more optimistic at *Islands/An International Magazine*. Editor Joan Tapper says that the postman brings her an average of fifty manuscripts and queries a month. She usually gives go-aheads to "more than one but less than five," but not often are any of these full-length features. They're more likely to be short items for the magazine's "Logbook" department.

Islands and *Los Angeles Magazine* are only medium-sized circulation publications (between 80,000 and 250,000 circulation). As circulation size increases, so generally does the number of competitors. Since there is a high positive correlation between circulation size and payment to writers, one reason for the big books' bulging mailbags is obvious. But there are others. Top pros like the exposure. Having their by-lines in front of lots of readers and lots of editors helps ensure that they'll stay in demand. Established writers who haven't yet reached the $20,000-plus income bracket look at the big magazines as the important step up.

But why do unpublished writers try to tackle the publishing world's Goliaths? First of all, these magazines' widespread visibility makes them the ones beginners know about. And secondly, beginners underestimate the difficulty of making those initial sales. Ask any group of beginning writers to list the magazines they plan to submit their articles to. Chances are, the lists will be almost identical—*Woman's Day*, *Family Circle*, *Reader's Digest*, *Sports Illustrated*, with an occasional *McCall's*, *National Geographic*, *TV Guide*, and *Good Housekeeping*—all magazines in the top twenty.

Added to the trials that even top-selling writers must face are the editorial boards of the big magazines. A proposal has to make a hit not only with one editor, but with the whole gang. At *National Geographic*, the article selection process goes something like this, according to Senior Associate Editor Joseph Judge: "A planning council made up of nine editors from the technical and picture sides of the magazine meets monthly to consider approximately fifty ideas—survivors out of a batch of several hundred. They may approve one or two."

In the case of sponsored magazines such as those put out under the auspices of automobile clubs or insurance companies, the editor almost always must have client approval before assigning articles. Client approval may involve one of the sponsoring company's officials or several of them. An editor friend laughingly tells about one publication she edited that included recipes—all of which had to be okayed by the client's wife.

Sounds hopeless? Not at all. Remember that we've been talking about high-profile, big and medium-sized magazines, the publications most writers submit articles to. There are some ten to fifteen thousand others out there, and that's not counting most trade journals and company publications. Many of their editors await mail time almost as eagerly as they do their annual vacations.

You won't find most of these magazines on the newsstands. But you may see them in your doctor's or insurance agent's office, or perhaps on a friend's coffee table. Some are distributed only abroad. Others are sent to members of a specific organization, club, church or profession.

Throughout the United States, lots of freelance writers support their families writing for magazines most of us have never heard of. And that's the secret. Their editors aren't being deluged by mail. So when these editors find competent writers who know how to produce what they want for their publications, those writers are kept busy full time.

It's encouraging, too, to listen to the reasons one typical editor gives for the majority of his rejections: " 'Does not fit our current editorial needs' from my magazine's point of view can be translated to read everything from impossibly sloppy manuscripts to dull writing to an idea that's been beaten to death. *But most often it means that any idiot should know we don't ever use the kind of material he's sent us*." (Italics mine.)

Barbara Gillam, travel editor at *Glamour*, adds, "Beginning writers think that there is some all-purpose article that any publication should be dying to print. Nothing could be further from the truth."

You can do better than that. There's no excuse for sending your work to a magazine where it hasn't a hope for publication, especially when you realize that successful manuscript submission depends on more than good writing and luck. Analysis allows you to deal with a stacked deck, and in-depth knowledge of the markets becomes your trump card. Since there are so many possible outlets for the writer's wares, every conceivable topic and individual writing style has its place. But in order to find that place, you have to know that it exists.

And the time couldn't be better for finding publications whose writing personalities are compatible with your own. For not only are we living in an era of extraordinary change — in life-styles, political systems, personal philosophies, technological advances — we're also in the midst of a veritable information explosion. So whenever there's a new sport, a new trend in eating, a new kind of career or business, a new area of technology, there's certain to be a new magazine (or magazines) to tell all about it.

As a result of the fact that these attitude and life-style changes, geopolitical events, environmental concerns, inventions and so on are translated into multiple forms of action, perceived from various viewpoints, and reacted to in a variety of ways, the number of article ideas they can generate is enormous.

A case in point is the home computer. Consider that no magazines aimed at the owners (or potential buyers) of personal computers were listed in the 1981 edition of *Writer's Market*. Ten years later, under the Personal Computer heading, *Writer's Market 1991* listed twenty. I counted eighty different magazines devoted to the subject at a local software store, and though you can say that most of them are aimed at the same audience, there are enough differences between them to see that their editors are each targeting a special segment of the computer-owning/buying public.

Perhaps not as dramatic but equally obvious has been the expansion of an old category — women's magazines. Readers of the publications that all of us grew up with — *McCall's, Ladies' Home Journal, Woman's Day, Family Circle, Good Housekeeping, Redbook, Cosmopolitan, Vogue* and *Harper's Magazine* — have discovered that there are a lot more ladies' faces decorating the magazine racks these days. Newcomers include *Entrepreneurial Woman, Moxie, Mirabella* and a whole lot more. In fact, there are about twice as many mainstream women's magazines today — close to one hundred — as there were fifteen years ago.

For women have become a far more diverse lot than we were then, and our magazines reflect that diversity. Single women climbing the corporate ladder. Married women who own businesses. Mothers punching the supermarket time clock. First-time job holders. Women reentering the work force. They're all working women. Then throw size, age and color into the mix.

Substitute married for single, single for married. And don't forget full-time homemakers. Or the fact that most women who work outside the home have domestic duties as well. Almost all of them are interested in clothes and beauty care, in relationships and sex. Some of them are committed to fitness, others to do-it-yourself projects, organic gardening, social and political causes. The result is an array of magazines that runs the gamut from hard-line feminism to hard-core fashion and beauty, with most of them aimed at a specific segment of the female population.

Attempts to categorize these magazines into groups, such as that made by the *Wall Street Journal* in a December 1989 article, aren't very helpful. Their four categories—magazines such as *Mademoiselle* and *Seventeen* for women younger than twenty; for single, working women in their twenties and early thirties like *New Woman*, *Cosmopolitan* and *Self*; for stylish, urban women (*Vogue*, *Mirabella* and the like); and magazines such as *Ladies' Home Journal*, *Good Housekeeping* and *McCall's*, which are aimed at homemakers—are too simplistic for potential contributors. They also fail to take into consideration the vast differences between the magazines within their groupings.

Add to the publication proliferation several other types of magazines that didn't exist a decade ago. In *Writer's Market 1981*, headings like "Relationships," "Ethnic and Minority" and "Disabilities" weren't necessary because not enough magazines were published to warrant separate designation. Any that were published were listed under "Alternative Publications." Today, eighteen magazines are listed under "Relationships," twenty-five under "Ethnic and Minority," and eight under "Disabilities."

Consider, too, the burgeoning group of people over the age of fifty-five—the retirement crowd. A handful of publications was written for them in 1981. Now there are fourteen listed in *Writer's Market*, each with a slightly different focus.

And in the field of new sports, just look what's happened to snowboarding. Introduced only a few years ago, this combination of skiing, surfing and skateboarding has at least three different magazines about it already being published.

Each of the editors of these magazines has to be sure that *Senior* isn't confused with *Senior Life Magazine* or *Senior World of California* and that *Snowboarder* has a personality that is different from that of *Snow Board*.

When more than one of the thousands of specialized magazines is aimed at a very specific audience—say, squash players or potato growers—you can be sure that each publication's slant, degree of technicality, tone and style will be different from the others.

As a result of this specialization, the writer who decides upon a subject and then tries to find a suitable market can succeed by doggedly searching for a magazine to fit the idea. The proficient market analyst, on the other hand, has a much easier job. By being familiar with a variety of publications at the outset, he can formulate his ideas on the basis of what he knows a particular magazine is buying.

Beginning writers all too often believe that a writer merely writes and doesn't have to spend time on bookwork. They're wrong. Through the years, I've found that I am most successful when I spend at least 50 percent of my time on market research, bookkeeping and marketing articles. And I am not alone. Many writers estimate that they spend up to 60 percent of their working time studying the markets and marketing their output.

Study of the markets, because of the growing number and increasing diversity of publications, has become more and more complex. I find that my copy of *Writer's Market* becomes dog-eared by the time it's a few months old. Published yearly, the book contains thousands of listings of markets for freelance material. Since the publications are divided into categories such as religious, regional, hobbies, and the like, you needn't devour the whole volume to get the information you want.

Freelancers usually think of general circulation magazines when they look for article markets. They don't realize that company publications and trade journals are a larger, often equally lucrative outlet for their writing.

Although the names of several hundred trade journals are included in *Writer's Market*, you can find out more about them and about company publications by looking through *Ayer's Directory of Publications, Business Publications Rates & Data, Standard Periodical Directory, Ulrich's International Periodi-*

cal Directory, and *Working Press of the Nation*. They're available at most library reference desks.

Keeping an eye out for magazines you've not seen before will lead you to still other publications. I never pass a reception room without glancing to see what magazines are on the tables. It's also a good idea to check at a well-stocked newsstand every month or two, as new titles are continually appearing.

Bettering Your Odds

In writing for both general circulation and company publications, you'll give Lady Luck a hand by concentrating your efforts on the most salable types of articles. They are:

Personality Pieces

Perhaps the most popular article type, you'll see some sort of personality piece in almost every magazine—a profile about an Olympic sprinter; a question-and-answer interview with a Hollywood star; a day in the life of a leading cosmetic manufacturer; a roundup of miniinterviews with people (usually public figures or celebrities) telling about their most exciting valentine, their most cherished possession, their goals for the future; an article about the members of a rock group.

Personal Experience/Life Experience Pieces

These are human interest accounts of how you or some other person has solved a problem, survived an unusual situation, or experienced something out of the ordinary. You see these pieces every month in many magazines—the family that adopted a dozen racially mixed children, or the baby who didn't die from a usually fatal birth defect. Curiosity plus good interview and observational skills are important in order to keep both profiles and personal experience articles from being one-dimensional.

How-tos

How-tos come in several guises. The project how-to tells readers how to make (make over or repair) a tangible object—

remodeling your kitchen, repairing a carburetor, knitting a sweater. The writing is straightforward and doesn't demand great literary skill. It does, however, require an ability to explain processes clearly.

Personal problem/solution and the miscellaneous problem/solution (how a community, agency, business met a challenging situation) are the other most popular how-to types: how a recently widowed woman conquered loneliness; the case history of how a take-out pizza business increased sales while cutting costs; point-by-point advice on how to stick to your exercise regimen; tips from a celebrity or an expert on successfully combining a career and marriage are all highly salable forms of the personal problem/solution how-to. Miscellaneous problem/solution how-tos are usually written according to the same basic formats. During the past decade, the percentage of project how-tos has declined, while the how-tos dealing with solving personal problems have increased. As a result, new wrinkles on solving old problems, or old wrinkles on solving new ones should be best sellers for some time to come.

Travel Articles

It has been predicted by people in the know that travel will be the world's leading industry by the year 2000. Therefore, travel articles, which are increasing in popularity, should continue to do so. These pieces fall into the following groups:

1. The broad brush, which tells about many of an area's attractions. It's a once-over-lightly piece devoting a phrase, a sentence, or, at most, a paragraph to each of the featured destination's points of interest.

2. The place or event piece describes one specific tourist attraction or event in depth.

3. Roundups contain information about several events or places with a common theme, such as ethnic festivals or country gardens.

4. Specialty travel incorporates some specific hobby, activity or pastime with an area, such as Palm Springs golf or scuba diving in Bonaire.

5. Hard news is reportorial in style. You'll find most travel hard news in travel trade publications.

Business Articles

You don't have to be a Harvard Biz School grad to write business pieces. But you must be accurate and willing to do your research thoroughly. Most salable types of business articles are about new products, how-tos, profiles, hard news, case histories, exposés, and anatomies of particular businesses or industries. You'll not only find business pieces in magazines like *Indiana Business* and *Western Investor*. You'll see them in newspaper Sunday supplements, general interest magazines, regional publications, retirement magazines, and magazines aimed specifically at women. In fact, it's in this latter category that an increasing number of articles have a business angle as a greater number of women are in business and acquire capital.

Humor is funny—it takes a special talent to put words on paper and make people laugh. When we speak humorously, we rely more upon voice inflection than most of us realize, and we choose our subject matter to fit the occasion as well as the people we're talking to. The written word doesn't transmit humor as readily. There are also wide differences in what people think is funny. Not only is humor highly subjective, the well-written variety is in short supply. So if you can make an editor chuckle, you're almost sure to make a sale.

Inspirational pieces must be crafted subtly in today's sophisticated market. You must uplift the reader's spirits and make your point without preaching. Since writers of inspirational pieces often use material objects to relay a spiritual message—budding trees symbolizing rebirth or new beginnings, a fork in the road representing choices that must be made—the writer who can come up with fresh analogies or new twists on old themes will find a welcome place in this field.

As you analyze markets and article types, don't neglect to analyze your own writing strengths and interests. Those will determine what kinds of articles you will write best.

The successful writer is the one who keeps abreast of the types of articles and subject matter currently in demand. She does this by becoming intimately acquainted with as many magazines as she can. Most successful freelancers read between twenty and sixty magazines a month.

Reading writers' magazines is another essential of market analysis. Their marketing news will keep you posted on editorial changes, names of magazines about to begin publication, and current needs of existing publications.

While you're working to tip the odds in your favor, remember that you'll beat a lot of the competition off the starting blocks simply by preparing a professional-looking submission. That means including a self-addressed envelope with sufficient postage to cover the cost of sending an answer to your query or returning your article. It means, too, that queries should be typed on plain white, regulation-sized paper or letterhead—no handwritten letters on memo pads or kitten-decorated notepaper. Although most professionals now use word processors, a typewriter is perfectly acceptable if the ribbon is new. Manuscripts should be neatly and accurately typed on $8\frac{1}{2} \times 11$-inch white computer or noncorrasable typing paper (see chapter nine for additional instructions on manuscript preparation).

Foolproof Filing

Keeping track of all the freelance markets that use the kinds of material you write would be a much bigger job than following all the stocks listed on the New York Stock Exchange. So, like the intelligent stock market analyst, study only the markets that hold the most potential for your success. To make the job easier, I compile minidossiers on each one.

The system is simple. You begin by making a list of the twenty or thirty magazines you would most like to write for. Your list should include publications you actually read and those with subject matter of interest to you. Whenever you read an article and say to yourself, "I could write as well as (or better than) that," you've found another indicator pointing to market possibilities.

Set up a file for each magazine and begin filling it with a photocopy of the publication's listing in *Writer's Market*. Underline information such as word length, the kinds of material the editors say they need, whether a query is necessary, or if finished articles are preferred. Note whether simultaneous submissions are welcomed or shunned; what size photos (if any) are asked for and if they should be black and whites, color transparencies, or a combination of the two. If the magazine isn't listed in *Writer's Market*, get that information, or as much of it as you can, from other sources.

You'll also want to take note of the rate of pay and whether that payment comes on acceptance or publication, as well as if there is a "kill fee" paid if the article is assigned and not used. These factors will be important to you in judging a market's desirability. Since payment on publication means that you'll see your check only after the magazine containing your article has gone to press (and sometimes long after), you've no guarantee that the article will be used and you'll ever be paid. Your editor may be replaced by one who doesn't like the piece. The magazine might go out of business. Your manuscript may lie forgotten in a file. There are all sorts of horrendous things that might—and do—happen between the time a writer is informed that his or her work is accepted and the "on publication" day, so it's wise where possible to pursue markets that pay on acceptance.

Another factor you'll want to take into consideration and make a note of when choosing a market is the kind of rights purchased. Most magazines today purchase "First North American Serial Rights," which means that after a work is published, the author can resell it as a reprint. When a publication insists on buying "All Rights" and the writer agrees to the arrangement, he gives up the chance to resell the work to any other market.

Include information about the form in which your target editors want to receive submissions. Some editors prefer triple-spaced manuscripts, while others want them double-spaced. There are still other magazines whose guidelines stipulate a certain number of characters to be typewritten on each line, or certain width margins. Include this information in your file.

Editors also have preferences as to the type of query they receive. Occasionally, an editor will prefer telephone queries (most often followed by an expansion of the proposed idea in writing). Other editors like what is called the "article outline," "article memo" or "query memo." Though the exact form may vary, this is essentially a piece of 8½ × 11-inch paper on which the first two or three paragraphs of the actual lead are double-spaced, followed by a single-spaced paragraph or two in which the writer conveys, in capsule form, essential elements of the entire article. Indicated also are the point of view to be used, some of the writer's sources, conclusions, and occasionally a complete anecdote or pertinent statistics. In most instances, whatever an editor's pet query form may be, a traditional query letter will do the job if it's well written and your idea is a good one.

Whenever you see an item about the publication in a writers' magazine or come across anything written by its editor, date, clip, and save it in your file. Bits of trade talk, such as editorial changes and which magazines aren't paying their writers promptly, are especially helpful.

I have found that your chances of acceptance are decreased if you query a magazine that has been recently written up in a writers' magazine. It's better to clip out the blurb, file it in the dossier, and query six months later. Why? Because just about every freelancer from Fairbanks to Forest Hills reads those items, and they all query at once. The note I received from Dorothy Harvey, former editor of *Capper's Weekly*, is typical of responses most writers receive to postpublicity queries: "Sorry to be so slow in replying, but we've been swamped with freelance material the past few weeks following mention in *Writer's Digest*." The note went on to say that while my idea was an interesting one, the magazine was overstocked with material.

Make note of any gossip you might hear about the magazine from other writers. Writers' conferences and club meetings are good sources of information, as long as you're able to sort out fact from disgruntled writers' fantasy.

Send for a sample copy of the publication and its guidelines for writers. Some magazines will send a single mimeographed page; others, several pages of information. One of the most complete writers' guidelines I've seen is put out by *Southern Outdoors* magazine. It is a twelve-page brochure that gives tips on everything from what kinds of photos to include to the magazine's taboos. Especially helpful is a section called "Keys to Writing the Saleable S.O. Story," a series of thirteen bulleted topics, such as tense, anecdotes, parochialism and attribution, that tell exactly what the editor is looking for. For example, under Parochialism: "We use the words 'South,' 'Southern' and 'Dixie' to remind readers that *Southern Outdoors* is a magazine devoted to them and the outdoor activities of their region. Your article must have a Southern focus and flavor, and its sources should be residents of the South." Though other magazines' guidelines may not be as illuminating, it's imperative that you have them in your reference file and follow them to the letter.

After you've sold an article to a publication, ask the editor about deadlines. Are they two, four, six months prior to the date of an issue's publication? Put that information in your file. Then, if you have an idea for a seasonal article, you'll know the optimum time to query about it. Knowing deadlines will also let you aim your queries so they won't hit the editor's desk when he or she is busiest and therefore least receptive to your ideas. This is especially important when querying magazines with small staffs, where closing dates could supply material for a five-hour-long Excedrin commercial.

Your files will never be completed unless you decide to write off a magazine as a lost cause or hang up your typing shoes. You will keep adding correspondence from editors of the magazines, pertinent articles that appear in them, and best of all, copies of manuscripts their editors buy from you.

The value of these minidossiers is obvious. They eliminate the precious minutes you would otherwise spend pawing through ten years' back copies of a writers' magazine ("I knew there was something about it somewhere") and trying to remember if it was Editor A who advised you to query again in six months. Files will keep your marketing information organized and will unmuddle your mind.

Targeting at Dollar Signs

Most writers wrestle with the question of whether to aim first for publications that pay top rates or to begin with those at the bottom. There are freelancers who are convinced that beginning writers should start near the bottom, trying for markets that pay two or three cents a word. And, of course, there are those who would have you start at the top. Then there's a third school of thought that says you should write for magazines you enjoy reading, regardless of what they pay.

Whose advice do you follow? I'd like to suggest that you analyze the subjects you enjoy, your areas of expertise, and your writing ability. Then try for publications that print the sort of material you are capable of producing. There's no harm in starting at the top if you're able to stand up to lots of rejections. Just because you start at the bottom does not mean you will be typecast and have to write for them forever. It is most important to send your queries and manuscripts to magazines whose formats they fit. And although Dr. Samuel Johnson said that no man but a blockhead ever wrote except for money, you may decide it's worth sending your work to magazines that pay only in copies, because having the publishing credit can be valuable, too.

Finding Your Place

Don't be discouraged if it takes some time to find your niche in the writing world. The subjects or magazines you choose now may prove less rewarding than those you concentrate on as your marketing knowledge and writing skills increase. Life circumstances, too, may affect your choices.

Judy Babcock Wylie began her working life as Advisor of Student Activities/Cultural Program at Ohio University while she was working toward her Ph.D. During the next six years, while she held a similar positions at the University of Arizona, Wylie wrote an occasional feature article and for two years wrote a column for a San Francisco home improvement guide.

Then she took a job at California State University at Los Angeles. "After three or four months, I was looking for a rev-up vacation," she says, "saw ads for health spas—there weren't many in 1977—and went to one for a week with a friend.

"We came back feeling wonderful, so we decided to try another spa next vacation. But we couldn't find any guides to spas." So Wylie decided to write one. The same month she signed a contract to be assistant to the university's vice president, she received a contract from Crown to write the book.

"It scared the hell out of me," she says. "I didn't know if I could write a book." But with sales of the book and calls from magazine editors asking her to write articles on spas as encouragement, Wylie took a year's leave of absence to write full time. She never went back; instead, she broadened her writing focus and now writes for top publications, including *Travel & Leisure*, the *Los Angeles Times*, *New Woman* and *Self*.

Duane Newcomb, a freelancer with thousands of articles to his credit, first chose camping travel as his specialty because of an educational background in forestry. Five years as owner of a retail store and a solid knowledge of business publications led him to change his focus, and he began writing trade articles. During the past few years, his emphasis has shifted to writing books, many of them guides to making money, which came as an outgrowth of his business article days.

Margo Hammond started working for the local newspaper during summers when she was in college studying political science. After graduation, she had a variety of jobs with newspapers — as an editor/writer at the *Washington Star*, a New York correspondent for a Portuguese newspaper, editor of the *Baltimore Sun Magazine*, and as an editor/reporter with the *Asian Wall Street Journal Weekly*.

"Always rather eclectic," she says, "I did everything from analyzing Japanese stock markets to writing personality profiles and destination pieces." When Hammond decided to strike out on her own as a full-time freelance writer, she retained her eclecticism with an international thread. Her articles, for such publications as *Connoisseur* and *McCall's*, have followed the Cleveland Symphony on a concert tour through Poland and Russia, looked at aboriginal art in Australia, and told about the richest little girl in the world, Athena Onassis. Hammond also writes a New York Times Syndicate column on hotels.

Dissatisfaction with the kind of religious education her five children were getting started Celia Scully writing. After selling a few pieces, she studied the markets and found that nonreligious publications that used family life and health-related articles offered wider opportunities and paid more money. Since her husband is a physician, access to ideas and interviews in these fields made them logical choices.

Then, one day, Scully received a phone call from the editor

of a magazine for travel agents asking her to cover a regional convention of agents to be held the next week in her town. That assignment led to a contributing editorship with the magazine. It also gave her the impetus to investigate other potential markets for the travel writer.

But after a few years of writing for top travel magazines, including *Travel & Leisure* and *Travel-Holiday*, Scully decided she preferred writing about health-related subjects, although she still does an occasional travel piece.

The secret of these writers' success has been their willingness to do the pick-and-shovel, unglamorous groundwork that lays the foundation for article sales and their willingness to take advantage of opportunities as they come along. Those opportunities will come along for you, too. They're waiting in the millions of blank pages editors must fill in their forthcoming issues. All it will take for you to provide the copy they need is a good measure of well-spent time — that preparation some people call "luck."

Chapter Two

What's Up Front

The past is but the beginning of a beginning.

H.G. Wells

Since Americans go for products in slick packages, editors know that a magazine's packaging—its front cover—is what attracts magazine stand browsers. Whether the reader's taste runs to souped-up Lamborghinis or a plateful of pilaf and prawns, that first visual impression, plus the blurbs advertising what is inside, determines whether he will walk away without buying or turn back to have a second look.

It's no wonder, then, that the writer ought to take a second look (and a third and fourth) at the covers of magazines she hopes to sell articles to. The pictures tell a lot. The words say even more, both in terms of the audience the editor wants to reach and the kinds of articles he or she is eager to buy.

For years, each of the established magazines has gone with the same type of cover, issue after issue, with only minor changes. If you want proof, just look at any issue of *National Geographic* from the 1950s. By comparing it with a current copy, you could tell it was a *Geographic* even if the name weren't there. You recognize the cover drawing without the *New Yorker* logo, and the red-bordered cover of *Time*. It's not that publishers are in a rut. They want their magazines to be readily recognizable. And editors of new publications realize that one way to become established fast is to come up with an attractive cover format that's identifiable as the magazine's own, setting it apart from the competition.

This competition is perhaps most ferocious in the field of women's publications, where editors are fighting tooth and painted fingernail to keep circulation rates climbing as a chorus line of newcomers comes onstage each month. At first glance, these women's magazines seem pretty much the same. After all, most of them feature women on the covers, don't they? Despite the magazines' proclivities for female faces (though the two big supermarket sellers, *Woman's Day* and *Family Circle*, prove that chocolate mousse and patchwork quilts sell magazines, too), you'll find that each cover girl's message is more than just a pretty face. *Ladies' Home Journal* cover choices run to celebrities like Barbara Bush and Princess Di. The models on *Shape*'s and *Self*'s covers exude the radiant health that comes from jogging five miles a day and taking your aerobics classes seriously. The models on the covers of *Working Mother* are usually dressed for the office and accompanied by offspring.

You'll never find a child on *Entrepreneurial Woman*'s cover, though, where the models' suits say "we mean business." *Lear's* cover models look older and more sophisticated than those on most women's magazines, and quality drips from every pore. *Vogue*'s ooze style. *Good Housekeeping* pictures celebrities or fresh-looking models, with a small photo or two of a second celebrity and fancy dessert or craft tucked among the article blurbs. And so it goes. Each magazine projects a cover image consistent with the kind of material its readers will find inside. When a homemaker picks up a copy of *Woman's Day*, with its familiar bouquet of spring flowers or remodeled kitchen on the cover, she expects to find the sort of articles, recipes and decorating tips she's come to associate with the magazine. So the editors serve up the same mix of editorial fare time after time and present it in the same kind of package.

It's too often been said that a picture is worth a thousand words. But the words on a magazine's cover can be worth a thousand pictures if you internalize what they're trying to tell you, the writer. Just below the magazine's name, there's occasionally a line of smaller, easily ignored type. It spells out just who that magazine is for, who sponsors it, or something about the publication's size: *Connoisseur*—"The Guide to the Civilized World"; *Compass*—"The Best Western International Travel Magazine"; *Black Belt*—"World's Leading Magazine of Self Defense"; *Success*—"The Magazine for Today's Entrepreneurial Mind"; *Itinerary*—"The Magazine for Travelers with Physical Disabilities"; *Gold Prospector*—"The Magazine of Mining *Adventure*" (italics mine); *New Age*—"Rethinking the Way We Live."

It's true that many magazines don't have that line of small print, but there is rarely one around today whose cover picture isn't punctuated by blurbs. Since the cover is the magazine's billboard, those blurbs are the lures. To the customer who hasn't read a particular magazine before or buys it only occasionally, these previews of what's inside are there to persuade him or her that the issue is worth its cover price.

One group of magazines on which you'll generally see fewer of these "come-hither" lines of type are those devoted to food. As a rule of thumb, the more obvious a food magazine's name, the less likely it is to have a tag line or a lot of cover blurbs. *Chocolatier*, for example, needs only the mouth-watering photo of a batch of brownies or a chocolate souffle and prospective readers get the message. However, *Cooking Light*—even with its tag line, "The Magazine of Food and Fitness,"—uses blurbs to explain what kind of food and fitness it's concerned with. The editor wants you to know that articles like "When the Grilling is Easy" and "How to Stick with Exercise" are inside.

Blurbs also have their function on the sponsored magazine that doesn't need these enticements to sell newsstand copies. Airlines want you to be so intrigued by the contents of their inflight magazines that you'll read them rather than put them back in the seat pocket after glancing at the cover. Motor club magazines and many of the insurance company-sponsored publications carry advertising inside them that their sponsors want you to see, so the editor uses the blurbs as a come-on. For sponsored publications (sometimes called custom-published magazines), in addition to giving their readers information and entertainment, usually have additional missions: product marketing, use of the product and public relations.

Cover lines shout loud and clear which articles the magazine's editor believes will attract the most readers. Chances are good that article ideas along the same general lines on related or parallel themes are the ones that the editor will receive most favorably in the future.

They will also tell you in no uncertain terms about the publication's slant, the conception a magazine has of its reader's interests and the role it wants to fill in their reading. This conception evolves from the editors' knowledge of the probable educational level of their magazine's readers, their economic levels, the magazine's own taboos, sacred principles and style, along with a variety of other editorial preconceptions. It's up to you, the writer, to detect a magazine's self-concept. Discerning the differences an editor sees between his or her publication and its competitors will result in sales.

Contrast these blurbs from a cover of *Gentlemen's Quarterly*—"Shape Up with Olympic Hopefuls," "The Best Clothes for Work & Play," "Bobby Brown's Flamboyant Style," "A Traitor in the Drug Wars," "The Most Beautiful Girl in the World," "Bucky Dent Against the Wall" and "Arnold (Schwarzenegger)—Fit for Fatherhood"—with these, which were on the cover of *Men's Workout* for the same month: "Push-Ups for Power," "Flexibility Training," "Barbell Basics," "The Road to Chiseled Abs," "Stretching Anytime, Anyplace" and "Cycling Fashions." Or these cover blurbs for *Men's Health*: "Age Erasers," "Burn Off Your Pot Belly," "New Hope for Blown Discs," "Prescription Aphrodisiacs" and "Vasectomy Reversal."

Now, it's entirely possible that the same man would read all of these magazines. But in regard to the magazines' slants and articles their editors think of as grabbers, an article that would fit like the weightlifter's tights on the one wouldn't cover the prescribed territory for the other.

Finally, the cover will tell you the magazine's price and how frequently it is published; for example, January-February usually means it comes out bimonthly, and Fall indicates a quarterly publication. Price is an important indicator when the magazine is extremely expensive. People who are willing to pay ten dollars and more for a magazine won't want to read about cost cutting.

In the course of your magazine analysis, you'll ultimately want to put together a reader profile for each of the magazines you would like to submit articles to. The cover is a logical starting point. As you look at its illustration and read the blurbs, ask yourself, What makes the typical reader who's attracted by this cover tick? Play amateur psychiatrist and probe his or her needs, dreads, unfulfilled wishes, and fantasies (for more information on reader profiles, see chapter three).

Casing the Contents

When you have gleaned every possible bit of information from the magazine's cover, turn a page or two until you come to the table of contents. Titles of a magazine's past articles provide one of the most successful mechanisms for generating article ideas to excite its editor. When I study back copies, I'm especially conscious of the kinds of pieces that seem to predominate in issue after issue. Are they mostly how-tos, informational, personal experience? Does the editor like a profile or two each month, or are all the articles essentially personality pieces?

If you've the time and a dogged determination to succeed, copy down the titles from three, four or five years of back issues. Patterns will emerge. The publication may *always* include a piece on wild turkey hunting in its August issue, family travel in April, or tips on avoiding colds in November. Perhaps there's a traditional piece on patriotism in July, back to school articles in September, or outdoor entertaining in June — you'll not only get article ideas but information on submission timing as well (at least six to eight months in advance for seasonal articles).

Getting in Focus

If you study the titles of articles, you'll be able to determine their scope, to tell whether they deal with broad subjects, several aspects of a subject, or a very narrow, sharply defined segment. You'll want to sharpen your focus when you analyze the articles themselves, but the titles alone can often tell you a great deal. By way of illustration, look at this one: "The Amazing World of Plant Genetics." That subject is very broad. Now consider "Cross-breeding — The Way to Increase the World's Food Supply." We're still talking about plant genetics but limiting the scope of the subject to a marked extent. "Hybrids in Your Garden" narrows it more, and "The Newest Field Corn Hybrid" cuts it still further.

It's rare that a magazine's breadth of focus is consistent in all the articles it prints, but as a rule of thumb you'll find more broadly focused articles in general interest magazines, more sharply focused pieces as the degree of specialization of the magazine increases. "The Amazing World of Plant Genetics," for example, might appear in a general interest magazine, an airline in-flight, a fraternal publication, or in any number of magazine categories. The piece on crossbreeding would fit into almost as large a variety of publications. "Hybrids in Your Garden" would appeal to yet a smaller audience, and it's doubtful whether "The Newest Field Corn Hybrid" would sell to any magazine other than one aimed at people in agribusiness.

Take any subject—the environment, exercise, exhaustion— and think of it as a pie. As you study titles, ask yourself if you're looking at that whole pie, a large piece, a medium-sized portion or a sliver.

There are clues on the contents page to the depth of treatment an editor prefers, too. By determining the number of pages in a piece and coordinating that information with the breadth of focus, you'll be able to get some idea of how deeply the magazine's writers delve into a particular topic. Since the amount of art accompanying articles varies so greatly, and many pieces are continued in columns at the back of the book, you'll want to get a rough word count by looking at the articles themselves.

Masthead Messages

At some point in your analysis, locate the magazine's masthead (the listing of members of the editorial staff, editorial and advertising office locations). First, check the masthead to see if the magazine is published by a sponsoring organization. Adele Malott, editor of *Friendly Exchange*, which is sponsored by Farmers Insurance, says, "I am continually amazed at the number of manuscripts we receive about other insurance companies." Even if the cover of the magazine (which says "The Magazine of the Farmers Insurance Group of Companies") were torn off, all the writers would have to do to avoid making this mistake is to take a look at the masthead, which says "Your copy of *Friendly Exchange* magazine is sent to you at the request of your Farmers Insurance Group Agent."

If it's feasible, tear the masthead page out and place it alongside the contents; if not, make a photocopy so you won't have to keep flipping pages. The masthead and contents pages together serve as your chances-of-success calculator.

The masthead gives the name of the current editor and in many cases tells you which department editor to submit your material to. A friend of mine, formerly assistant editor of a medium-sized magazine, once characterized her office as "a perpetually revolving door." The magazine had five different editors in a period of three years, and the assistants were either shifted or replaced with mind-numbing regularity. This isn't an isolated example. I write for one magazine that is on its sixth editor in seven years. Several have had three during the same period.

Although a few editors have been at the same desk for decades, by and large editing is an extremely mobile profession. Publications like *Writer's Market* and other market listings often have gone to press just as an editor resigns, so you should always check current issues of the publications to see who is editor. Address your correspondence to that person. Never, ever, begin a query or a cover letter with "Dear Sir."

Compare the article by-lines with names of staff members to find out how many of an issue's pieces were written by freelancers. In a magazine of from fifty to one hundred pages it's an easy task to tell which of the articles were written by staff or by contributing editors. A bigger magazine with a large staff takes more time. But this step of the process is essential, as the following notes I took from one issue each of *Friendly Exchange*, *Motorland* and *Discovery* will show.

Friendly Exchange: 8 articles with by-lines
    0 by staff members (or authority with staff member)
    8 apparently by freelancers

Motorland: 7 articles with by-lines
    4 by staff members
    3 apparently by freelancers

Discovery: 5 articles with by-lines
   0 by staff members
   5 apparently by freelancers

I qualify the number of articles by freelancers with the word "apparently" for good reason. Many of the smaller publications have editorial staffs of two or three people. Some are even one-person operations. Editors often want to, or have to, write several articles that appear in a single issue. They're reluctant to let the world know how short staffed they are, what a skimpy budget they're forced to work with, or how much they love to see their own words in print, so they write under other names. One editor writes under five different pseudonyms (both male and female) that I'm aware of. Several others I know use one or two pen names. This practice isn't so common in the big publications' editorial offices, but it does happen, so be aware that the articles may be more heavily staff-written than your statistics indicate.

I don't ever let the "apparently" qualification stop me from submitting, even though I suspect some of the by-lines are fictitious. Who knows? The staff may have been forced to write pieces simply because they couldn't find the kinds of material they wanted in their submission piles.

While I'm studying the names of the freelancers, I put a check mark opposite those whose work I've seen before in the magazine or remember from other publications. Writers whose names appear frequently in a magazine I assume to be in the editor's "stable," writers relied upon through the years who are thought of first when the editor makes assignments. They have the inside track, since they're known quantities, and they write the bulk of the articles for a great many publications. One magazine I write for publishes about forty articles each year (it appears quarterly). Of those, I have written as many as six during a twelve-month period and I know, by reading the by-lines, that there are a couple of freelancers who contribute as many or more.

Don't let the appearance of these regulars keep you from submitting to a magazine, for a successful sale or two might find you a stall in that stable, too. But if you find, upon studying six or more back issues of a magazine, that almost every by-line belongs to a staffer, contributing editor, regular contributor, or big name, you'll probably want to write that particular publication off your list of prospects. The competition is just too tough to waste your energies on. The exception here is if you have an article idea that's perfect for that particular magazine and that only you can write. In general, however, concentrate on those magazines that buy most of their articles from freelancers.

The masthead often includes the names of contributing editors who are authorities in their particular fields. This information is valuable in weighing a certain article's chances. If you have a great slant for an astrological article, for instance, but one of the contributing editors has written several books on astrology, you'll have more success contacting an editor who doesn't have an astrologer on standby. Since many magazines are strong on articles authored or coauthored by experts, check the contents page to see if you'll need the collaboration of one on your proposed piece. If all personal relationship or mental health pieces, for example, have an authority's name as part of the by-line, it's likely that the editor won't even consider an article without one.

Now, let's go back to *Friendly Exchange*, *Motorland* and *Discovery* to size up their relative desirability as markets. Each is a sponsored magazine. *Friendly Exchange* and *Discovery* come out quarterly, while *Motorland* is a bimonthly. *Discovery* pays the highest rates (the usual range for features is $800-plus, according to *Writer's Market*). The person who makes out the writers' checks at *Motorland* says that she has never sent out a check for more than $800 for both text and photos, and that payment starts at about $300. Editor Malott of *Friendly Exchange* says her publication pays $300 to $800 an article.

Next, let's look at content. Seven of the by-lined articles in the issue of *Friendly Exchange* are travel pieces; one is not. According to the minibios that follow the articles, at least seven of the writers are established freelancers.

All three of the freelance articles in the issue of *Motorland* are on travel. There is no indication in the magazine of whether their authors have published previously, but the name of at least one of them would be recognized by writers who study the travel article market.

Of the five freelance articles in *Discovery*, four are travel articles and the other piece is on photography. The minibios indicate that two of the writers have written for *Discovery* before, and one is travel editor of a major metropolitan newspaper.

It's impossible to tell if the other two are first-timers or old hands, but I would guess that they are the latter, since the current staff at *Discovery* is known for generally going with writers they know, even if the other writers live in the very places they want articles about.

Putting all our information together, we see that though *Discovery* pays the highest rates, it's perhaps the toughest market to crack. *Motorland* publishes less than half the freelance pieces that *Friendly Exchange* does, but it is published six times a year as opposed to four. Even so, *Friendly Exchange*'s estimated thirty-two articles a year gives the competent writer a rather decided edge over *Motorland*'s estimated total of eighteen. And there's an exposure bonus here, too, as *Friendly Exchange*'s circulation of 4.6 million is one of the fifteen largest in the country.

Next, let's compare the three leading recreational vehicle magazines—*MotorHome, Trailer Life* and *Family Motor Coaching*—to see what happens.

MotorHome: 16 articles and columns with by-lines
    4 by staffers
    3 by contributing editors
    9 apparently by freelancers

Trailer Life: 14 articles and columns with by-lines
    3 by staffers
    0 by contributing editors
    11 apparently by freelancers

Family Motor Coaching: 30 articles and columns with by-lines
    1 by staffer
    0 by contributing editors
    29 apparently by freelancers

All three magazines are published monthly. *MotorHome* and *Trailer Life* pay from $250 to $500 for the complete package of article and photos, according to Barbara Leonard, Editorial Director. Robbin Maue, Assistant Editor of *Family Motor Coaching*, says her magazine pays a top of $225 for travel articles plus photos, $500 for technical pieces.

Five of the freelance articles in the issue of *MotorHome* are travel pieces; four are technical. One freelance piece in *Trailer Life* is about food, five are technical, four are travel related, and one is a how-to. In the issue of *Family Motor Coaching*, nineteen articles are about some facet of travel; four are informational; two, food related; two, technical; one, nostalgia; and one, how to.

Four of the articles in *Trailer Life* had the same by-line, indicating that this writer is a very frequent contributor to the publication. Of the *Family Motor Coaching* pieces, two articles were by one writer, two by another, and three by a third. There is no indication as to whether the other writers in any of these publications are first-timers or not.

Although *MotorHome* and *Trailer Life* pay more than *Family Motor Coaching* for travel and other nontechnical articles, pay for technical pieces is about the same. However, chances for the competent writer to have material accepted by the last of these are far greater since *MotorHome* buys approximately 108 freelance pieces a year, *Trailer Life* buys 132, and *Family Motor Coaching* buys 348.

There's even more we can learn from the mastheads of these publications that might further influence our market choice. We find that both *MotorHome* and *Trailer Life* are published by TL Enterprises in Agoura, California, and that *Family Motor Coaching* is the publication of the Family Motor Coach Association, with headquarters in Cincinnati.

This information in itself is important, because it's easier (and less expensive) for staffers to write articles that have to do with their own part of the United States. Since budget is always one of a publication's major concerns, and payment for articles generally is not dependent upon location of the place written about, it's easier to sell pieces about places that are too time-consuming and costly for the staff to write.

A contents/masthead bonus is finding articles written by the editor. You will definitely want to read, and perhaps reread, those to familiarize yourself with the phrases she likes, words he seems fond of; her slant, his structure. And if the article's subject has been treated in somewhat the same way as the subject you plan to write about, you'll want to include it in the group of pieces you plan to analyze. Some writers also suggest that if you know an editor occasionally freelances, it's worth your while to go to the library and check *Readers' Guide to Periodical Literature* and the computerized indexes such as Infotrack to see if any of her articles are listed. Analyzing them will give you added insights as to the format and style she likes.

Editors often confess that they're frustrated writers. One of them says she looks forward all year to the annual article she allows herself to write for the magazine she edits. Another admits that what he would rather be doing is freelancing. The only place most of them get to flex their pens instead of their blue pencils is on the editor's page. And then, alas, most of the readers skip over it. Don't *you* dare.

On these pages you'll see mention of authors who are new to a publication, as well as old-timers. This information will help you size up your chances, but the most important discoveries you'll make will be about the editors themselves. Of course, there's nothing quite like getting to know an editor face to face. But when that's impossible, getting to know one via the editor's page can provide an adequate substitute, for personality clues are sprinkled all about. When an editor writes about the articles that appear in the magazine, enthusiasm for particular pieces and photographs shows through. Some pages provide insights into the editor's philosophy of life. Others, such as those of *Travel & Leisure*'s Pamela Fiori, give us glimpses of their personal lives. Editors sometimes write about their favorite things or their pet peeves. As one editor says, "No freelancer can possibly know all of my magazine's taboos without knowing me. Some of those taboos have nothing at all to do with the magazine per se, but have everything to do with how I feel personally about certain subjects."

Reading editors' pages won't clue you in on the editorial decision makers' every enthusiasm, attitude or prejudice, but the information you garner will give you a definite advantage over your competitors. If you have an idea that dovetails with an editor's cherished cause or deepest concern, one promoting a favorite avocation or condemning a practice he deplores, you'll be well on your way to a sale.

You'll want to take note not only of what an editor says but of the way in which it is said. Then, when you're ready to write your query, you can fashion it in both the magazine's and the editor's image. Use some phrases she likes. If she's exhibited a penchant for short, punchy sentences, let your query sentences be short and punchy, too. Although you'll want to study the magazine's articles for style before you polish your proposal, analysis of the front pages will set the tone for what you write.

To give yourself an extra boost, read the letters to the editor. Pay attention to the kinds of articles that evoke the most response, for they're the kinds the editor will be looking for to keep interest up in forthcoming issues.

Chapter Three

Reading the Ads

You can tell the ideals of a nation by its advertisements.

Norman Douglas

*H*ave you noticed how often articles on updating your wardrobe are flanked by ads for pantyhose; pieces on do-it-yourself home repairs adjoin full-page advertisements for home workshop tools; an article called "Choosing the Perfect Pet" just happens to be next to an ad for cat food? Have you ever wondered why different ads for the same product appear in various magazines? Coincidence? Not on your editorial life.

Advertising revenues are what keep most magazines published. And there's almost always a direct relationship between the kinds of articles in a publication and the kinds of products that are touted in it. Therefore, it behooves every determined freelancer to become an expert in ad analysis. For the pictures with their persuasive pitches—usually comprising 40 to 60 percent of a magazine's pages—are worth more than a thousand words in directing the writer toward the kinds of articles that will make him a super-salesman.

Since Hammurabi ruled Babylon, two thousand years before Christ, advertising has been a part of business. The Babylonian barkers who shouted the virtues of their employers' wares have been replaced by more sophisticated methods of sales seduction. But the message remains the same—"Buy Me."

Magazines, along with newspapers, TV, and radio, are the manufacturers' and businessmen's media for proclaiming their products' tantalizing qualities. That's why it's so important for writers to find out about advertising's impact on editorial content in general, and on their targeted magazines in particular.

In order to understand how a magazine's ads affect—and are affected by—the articles it publishes, you must know how the ad-placing process works. It goes like this: Manufacturers and businesses know what kinds of people buy their products through customer surveys and feedback from their salespeople and dealers. Because advertising a product nationwide, regionally or even locally is a bigger job than the majority of companies care to handle within their organizations, most of them rely on advertising agencies.

The ad agency, with knowledge of what a product's users are like, determines which medium or combination of media will be most effective in reaching potential customers, then produces ads that will do the job of persuading. To do that job, the creators of the ads must know exactly to whom they are speaking. Top ad agency people, like successful freelance writers, have an extensive knowledge of individual magazines' readerships. They get this information from readership profiles provided by the magazines or from surveys contracted for or conducted by the agency itself.

These profiles are as different from one another as the magazines whose readers they describe. The profile that *Sunset Magazine*'s research people put out, for example, gives its readers' median household income figures, augmented by information on size of household; age, educational level, and occupation of head of household; length of residence in present home; estimated value of that home; and the number of readers who live in urban, suburban or rural areas.

Sierra, published by the Sierra Club, distributes a profile that, in addition to demographics, tells potential advertisers that 7 percent of its readers ordered pet supplies/accessories by mail/phone during the past twelve months (64 percent ordered clothing or shoes); 95 percent are involved in civic activities; 95 percent use national credit cards; 58 percent hold valid passports. By reading the profile you know what sports these people enjoy, how much they spend on film and developing, what kinds of consumer goods they own, and what other publications they read.

One of the most detailed readers' profiles I've seen is put out by *Scuba Times*, the second oldest scuba publication in the country. According to it, their average reader earns $53,100 a year and has a college degree. This average reader took eleven trips in the continental United States during the past twelve months and 2.3 trips outside the United States in the past three years, spending 7.8 days on the typical trip in the latter category.

He (the average reader is a married man, 34.5 years old) plans to take an international dive trip within the next twelve months and will spend an average of $2,126 on that trip; owns a 35mm camera and 1.38 boats at an average cost per boat of $10,213. This extensive profile goes on to report that 46.3 percent of subscriber households have at least two divers and that 52 percent are influenced by dive stores when choosing their diving destinations. More than 98 percent have valid passports or plan to obtain them within the next twelve months, and large percentages of them were asked by others within the past year about diving locations, equipment, certification and training.

Other magazines' media packets tell such things as the percentage of readers who have savings accounts and own common stocks, what their favorite forms of recreation are, the modes of transportation they use when traveling, and how they entertain.

Magazines don't use these profiles only as advertising tools. Through them, the editors get to know their readers and learn to cater to these readers' interests when choosing articles for publication. Since advertising is slanted toward a magazine's audience, by analyzing the ads you can see that readership through the editor's eyes.

You, as a freelancer, can use the advertising agencies' techniques in targeting your articles. It is possible, in many cases, to obtain a magazine's media packet by requesting it from the advertising department. But with or without this packet, you'll want to study the ads displayed in several issues of your chosen publication to find out more.

Who Gets the Message?

Ad analysis will do two things for you: 1) help you form an accurate idea of what the "typical" reader of a magazine is like (her interests, economics, hopes, and priorities), and 2) allow you to zero in on subjects the editors think will interest both readers and advertisers.

The first question to ask yourself as you analyze is what kinds of products are advertised — luxury items, necessities, gimmicks. Then look at the people in the pictures. Are they young, old, men of the world, sexy ladies? Do you get a mental image of readers who are matter-of-fact, intellectual, gullible? And what messages — both explicit and implicit — are the advertisers trying to communicate?

There's a world of life-style difference between the readership of a magazine whose ads show distraught mothers with water-spotted glassware, stained baseball jerseys, and mud-tracked floors and the magazine whose advertisements feature a succession of well-dressed women carrying eight-hundred-dollar briefcases.

You won't find much audience overlap between magazines whose advertisers include the National Rifle Association (NRA) and those advertising T-shirts saying "Save the Whales." Ads for home permanents and couturier fashions, top-of-the-line luggage and mail-order bartending courses, luxury hotels and beer-brewing kits won't appear in the same magazines unless their circulations are large.

You won't have much chance of selling a scholarly article to a magazine that goes in heavily for muscle-building and bust-development ads; or do-it-yourself pieces to publications whose advertisers sell Cartier bracelets, sterling silver adjustable collar stays, and Lladro porcelain. The editor of the first magazine, however, will most likely go for self-help articles that can make readers feel more desirable; the editor of the latter will be interested in pieces slanted toward affluent readers.

Let's get more specific and compare the ads in some of the women's publications. As a result of women's changing roles and life-styles, the number of magazines directed at them has grown tremendously during the past few years. Correspondingly, so has the diversity of their ads as well as their editorial matter.

Not only are these new magazines targeted toward women with specific interests — business, fitness, fashion — they're specifically aimed at definitive age groups (e.g., *Lear's* — for the Woman

Who Wasn't Born Yesterday) and socioeconomic groups.

Mirabella, for example, in a full-page subscription pitch in another Murdoch publication used this description of the magazine: "MIRABELLA doesn't pretend to be for everyone. But if you already have a definite sense of your own style and are satisfied only by the highest standards of quality and good taste, please join us."

Advertisers have been quick to capitalize on these targeted audiences. Large store chains or manufacturers will feature different clothes with different age-group models in various magazines. A leading beer manufacturer's full-page ad in some of the fashion/beauty magazines directed to the eighteen to thirty-five-year age group showed a couple of beauties (with a handsome man in the background) wearing the latest in bicycling gear and drinking its product in an appealing outdoor setting. That same manufacturer advertised its foundation to fight illiteracy with full-page ads in that month's issue of magazines aimed at the more sophisticated, business-oriented reader.

Cosmo's ads are, for the most part, sexually oriented. You'll see advertisements for at-home pregnancy tests, suncare products, cosmetics and perfumes, contraceptives, underwear, liquor and cigarettes. All these mirror an item in editor Helen Gurley Brown's column "Step Into My Parlor" in the February 1990 issue. She wrote, "Twelve thousand of you darling girls responded to a questionnaire in the October issue asking which COSMO features you enjoyed most. You enjoyed most (whew!) the ones we think we *do* best—the man-woman, sex, emotional articles. . . ."

The products advertised in *Glamour* and *Redbook* are usually in the mid-price range—cosmetics you can buy at the drugstore (not at the dime store or at an upscale department store), clothes from middle-market department stores, foods you can find in your local supermarket, cars like Mazdas, Hondas and Fords. Products advertised in *Vanity Fair* and *Vogue*, by contrast, are definitely upscale, with ads for such products as Chivas Regal and Mercedes Benz.

There are a number of fashion/beauty ads in *New Woman*, but you'll also see ads for telephone answering machines. Note, however, that very few ads feature foods or family-oriented products. In *Working Woman*, you'll not only find ads for answering machines, but for home computers as well, and several ads that are family oriented. Clothing that's advertised generally will be more classic and/or sophisticated than that in *New Woman*.

You won't see many clothing ads in *Entrepreneurial Woman*, however. Instead, it is loaded with ads for publications like the *Wall Street Journal*, for franchise businesses, calculators, cash registers and computer software.

Ads in *Victoria* are the antithesis of those in magazines aimed at working women. It may well be that *Victoria* subscribers work outside the home, but they don't buy the magazine to read about business. Without exception, the ads are romantic and/ or have to do with the Victorian era—Victorian dolls, Victorian notepaper, textiles and home furnishings with a Victorian flavor. Contemporary clothing that's advertised is very feminine, and full-page ads for paperback romances are in just about every issue.

Food ads, which are found in the majority of women's magazines, can provide a wealth of information, especially if they contain recipes. Notice whether these recipes are gourmet or traditional, complicated or fast and easy to fix. Are the ingredients common, inexpensive ones that every cook would have in the kitchen; are they fairly mainstream like kiwi fruit and artichokes, or downright exotic like sun-dried tomatoes, lemon grass and goat cheese? Pay attention, too, to whether they're slanted toward the health conscious.

Your analysis job will be easier if you make a checklist and enter your findings on it. You may have nothing to submit to a particular magazine until some time in the future. If you have the ad information in your file, it will come in handy at that later date. The checklist might look something like this:

1. What kinds of products are advertised?
   a. Necessities
   b. Luxuries
   c. Get-rich schemes
   d. Do-it-yourself aids
   e. Gimmicks
   f. Food

      g. Clothing
      h. Home furnishings
      i. Business-related products
      j. Beauty and health products
      k. Books, tapes and records
      l. Sporting goods
      m. Recreational equipment
      n. Trip destinations and tours
      o. Other
2. What age people are pictured?
      a. Children and infants
      b. Teenagers
      c. Young adults
      d. Middle-aged adults
      e. Senior citizens
3. What sort of people are they (professionals, blue-collar workers, athletes)?
4. What messages are the advertisers communicating?
      a. Pleasure, happiness
      b. Popularity, desirability
      c. Efficiency
      d. Style, beauty, handsomeness
      e. Prosperity, success
      f. Health
      g. Advancement of goals
      h. Helping others
      i. Problem solving
      j. Entertainment
      k. Security
      l. Other

There's a second type of advertising you will come across in many magazines — the mail-order ads. They are usually placed toward the back of the publication, generally printed in black and white, and include an order blank or mailing address. Aircraft preheater systems, leather moccasins, Christmas cards and mosquito repellant are only a few of the thousands of items marketed by this method, so don't overlook the clues they provide.

As you scrutinize the ads and note your findings, you'll see a readership profile emerging. The larger the publication's circulation and the more general its editorial content, the more facets that profile will contain. Study of specialized magazines with relatively small readerships will result in more sharply defined "typical" readers.

The Ad/Editorial Connection

The degree to which advertising influences the copy in a magazine depends both on the advertising agencies involved and the magazine's decision makers. Since advertising is often a magazine's lifeblood, editors use editorial copy as bait to entice potential accounts. They solicit these customers on the basis of articles they plan to run in upcoming issues. Their advertising salespeople approach a prospective client armed with a printed sheet that lists future articles, one or several of which are on subjects of interest to the people that client wants to present his message to.

Many agencies place their business with no strings attached. They agree to have a certain number of ads run at specified rates. Others stipulate in their negotiations that they will place the ads only if an article relating to the business or product appears in an issue of the magazine.

Most people with editorial power reject such proposals, but there are more trade-offs than you might imagine. And another, more subtle factor in choosing articles involves advertising. I have had editors come right out and tell me that they will buy certain travel articles I have proposed if their advertising departments can come up with sufficient advertising to support the pieces.

On the other hand, in cases where there has been no attempt at coercion or need to obtain advertising in order to run certain pieces, editors will frequently place ads in the layout where they will give their advertisers the most mileage. This is not as contradictory as it may sound. These editors' code of journalistic ethics says that they will not be forced into having advertisers dictate editorial copy, but it allows them voluntarily to position ads next to articles that will complement them.

To take advantage of any advertising/editorial content tie-ins, whichever way they have come about, it's a good idea every now and then to skim the pages of *Advertising Age, Adweek/ West*, or any other major advertising agency publications. These are the bibles of the ad agency trade. They tell who has landed what account and often give particulars on upcoming advertising campaigns, including (and this is what you want to know) the magazines in which the ads are scheduled to appear. Magazines switch roles and become the advertisers in these publications, with their ads often including readership profiles—another incentive for the freelancer to study them.

Whether there's an advertising/editorial content tie-in or not, one cardinal rule exists at all magazines. *Never antagonize an advertiser*. A leading car magazine in the early 1970s was asked to test-drive and report on a new model automobile. Their findings were negative, to say the least, and the car, surrounded by a pigpen, graced the magazine's cover. As a result, a former member of the staff says, the magazine lost $100,000 in advertising from the car's manufacturer. This incident was the Halley's Comet of the editorial world. It won't happen again for a very long time.

As a freelancer, you won't score points or sell articles by writing pieces that will deeply offend one of a magazine's big accounts. Editors are sensitive about advertiser alienation to the point that they will have their advertising people check out an even slightly questionable article with the advertiser before they will run it.

Sponsoring organizations have a very large say and tremendous veto power over the magazines put out under their auspices. Although the editor may be hired by a publishing company that is not a part of that organization, he and the publisher know that their existence depends on keeping their sponsors happy. If that sponsor is an automobile club, for example, they know that the magazine won't survive long on a diet of mass transit and anti-driving articles; in fact, a single issue with one such offending article will most likely result in someone else taking over at the wheel. By the same token, a publication sponsored by a travel credit card company won't be receptive to articles on cutting vacation costs by picnicking or camping.

In all cases, the sponsor's purpose must be advanced by the material that appears in its magazine. Usually, you can tell if a magazine is sponsored by looking at its cover or masthead, where the words "The Gulf Auto Club," "Official Journal of the National Geographic Society," or "Official Magazine of the Aircraft Owners and Pilots Association" are printed. The connection is not always so obvious. That's where examining the ads comes in. If you notice that many of the ads tout the same products (or causes) there's a good chance that the publication is linked, if not by outright monetary sponsorship, at least philosophically, with a sponsoring group.

If you have a year's back copies of a publication available for analysis, chances are you'll realize that like those of us who go on annual bathing suit diets, most magazines become skinnier during the summer months than at any other time of the year. Why? Because advertisers know that people spend more time outdoors and less of it reading than during the colder months. Thoughts of buying other than summer-use items are more appealing when there aren't so many other entertainment options.

The decrease in advertising means that there won't be as many pages of editorial copy either, since the amount of advertising determines how much space will be allotted for articles in most magazines. As a freelancer, you'll want to take advantage of this slimming and fattening cycle by submitting queries for nonseasonal material during summer and autumn when editors are thinking about production of the larger issues in the months ahead.

To illustrate the practical application of ad analysis, let's look at how an experienced freelancer puts her findings to work. This writer specializes in travel pieces and is planning a trip to Scandinavia, with visits to Norway, Denmark and Finland. She has collected back issues of several magazines that she knows from past study use material on foreign destinations. Since the Scandinavian countries have become a popular topic for recent travel articles, our writer must have fresh angles in order to make sales. To get ideas and choose the most likely markets, she begins studying the ads.

The first thing she notices is that all the magazines are appreciably thinner during summertime. This fits in nicely with late autumn queries, since spring is the time most travel editors use stories on Europe. Since the spring issues bulge with ads, the editors will be looking for a proportional amount of editorial copy.

One magazine's advertisements are heavily slanted toward

luxury—five-star hotels, expensive luggage, elegant silver. It also consistently carries advertising for art/antiques auction firms such as Sotheby's. People pictured in the ads look affluent and tend to be in their forties and fifties. The reader profile is clearly focused—mature readers who like and can afford high-quality merchandise and first-class travel.

The second magazine's ads are directed toward people who like to spend their leisure time out of doors. Backpacks, dehydrated foods, books on flora and fauna, and build-your-own sailboat kits are among the products advertised. The ads' models are young, robust-looking, and casually dressed.

According to the third magazine's ads, its readership consists largely of people with families, as many of them picture a parent or parents with their children. The kinds of goods and services offered for sale are in the mid-price range, with some do-it-yourself items.

When the writer has finished analyzing these three magazines, she has a list of more ideas than she will have time to use. The ideas for the first magazine include a piece on Hannah Ryggen tapestries and other Norwegian art treasures, buying Iittala glassware in Finland, and finding antiques in Copenhagen. Among her query possibilities for the second publication are pieces on Scandinavian foods that can be adapted to backpacking, picking wild berries in Norway, and camping in Finland's Aland Islands. The third magazine seems to be a natural for articles on what to do with the kids in Denmark, the Norwegian Coastal Voyage as a family vacation, and Finnish toys. Each of the magazines, the writer concludes, might also want pieces on shopping, restaurants/food or accommodations, slanted in their individual readership's direction.

By following the same analytical procedure with any magazine you'll be able to pinpoint the audience that you, and that important editor, want to reach. You'll never make editor-alienating mistakes like those Barbara Gillam, travel editor of *Glamour*, shakes her head over. "Anyone should know that articles on cost-cutting vacations for retirees aren't for us by looking at our ads," Gillam says.

Advertising pays, say advertisers. Advertising analysis, I'm convinced, will pay off for you.

Chapter Four

Looking at the Pictures

The concept of the photograph precedes the operation of the camera.

Ansel Adams, *The Print*, 1950

One of a magazine staff's jobs — a job that readers and many writers don't give a second thought to — is deciding how the magazine should look. There are considerations that go beyond making it attractive, like suiting the purpose of the magazine. A publication promoting tourism, for example, won't have pictures of the homeless illustrating its articles. Compatibility of stories on the same spread (two pages facing each other) and placement of continuations of articles to other pages must also be considered. Editors also strive to avoid conflict — an article on oil spills on the same page as the ad for an oil company just isn't politic.

Then there's the matter of consistency. The editor wants readers to feel familiar with his publication and that means laying out the material so that each article has commonalities with the others, not to the point of being boringly repetitious, but involving enough sameness to identify each page as being part of the magazine. Perhaps the editor almost always uses "kickers," those large boldface quotes from an article that punctuate the text. He or she may rely heavily on blurbs to hook readers into reading on. Picture captions may always be complete sentences or may merely be labels. Or there may be no captions at all. Then there are the pictures themselves.

Editors, ideally working in conjunction with art editors and designers, display their consistency most graphically in the kinds of pictures they choose. Therefore, the right photographs, as well as the right words, are what sell articles. I'm convinced many of my sales would never have been made if I hadn't supplied the pictures. Most freelancers proficient with both pen and camera agree. To quote one, "It's hard to say sometimes whether editors bought a piece because the pictures were there or the words were there; but most often it's because *everything* was there and they didn't have to do much more to get the piece ready to run."

It's easy to understand why most editors prefer to get text and photos in one simple-to-slip-into-an-issue package. Hiring a photographer to illustrate a story is expensive — she is paid not only the hourly rate but also travel expenses. Getting just the right pictures from a stock photo agency costs a lot, too, both in money and time the editorial staff has to spend on the project. Even rummaging through their own photo files takes valuable time. So the writer who is able to provide good photos gets the nod over another who has produced an equally appealing article sans illustrations.

Not only do most editors prefer that the writer supply photos, some of them require pictures since that's the only way they can obtain them. Outdoor and travel writers, especially, find that if they're doing pieces on fishing for Lake Ohrid trout or snowmobile races to the Hudson Bay, the availability of photos is what makes the difference between an acceptance and an "I wish I could buy it but . . . ."

If I were a crybaby, I could weep buckets over the pieces on Great Basin National Park and Montreal's underground shopping centers that didn't sell for the sole reason that I didn't have good enough photos to go with them. There's nothing so demoralizing as a letter from an editor that says, "I love the story, but the photos just aren't up to our standards." But instead of crying, I've resolved to never let it happen again.

Ideally, you have enough technical competence to take salable shots or are willing to learn. If for some reason you can't or don't want to combine photography and writing, you can team up with a freelance photographer on assignments. Or you may find that you are able to get the pictures you need from government agencies, travel bureaus, businesses, and other sources. You can ascertain whether the latter type of photos will do the job by reading the photo credits in back issues of your target magazine.

But before you load your camera or send those requests off to photo sources, investigate the magazine's basic photo requirements. Does it print only color, black and whites, or a combination of the two? It's futile to send black and whites to a publication that uses only color, and expensive (and therefore often not worth the expense) for a magazine to convert color to black and white. Does the editor want to see transparencies or 8×10-inch glossies or contact sheets? Many amateurs make the mistake of sending prints (color, Polaroid, or Instamatic) along with their manuscripts. Few magazines will consider using them.

Most editors/art directors will require your shots be captioned. The preferred way is typed on paper and attached with tape to the back of black and whites, listed on a separate sheet correspondingly numbered for transparencies. To get the specifics, write for the magazine's photo guidelines if they are available and check the requirements listed in *Writer's Market* and *Photographer's Market*.

However you obtain your photos, it's vital that you send your editor in-focus shots that click with the magazine's image. And that means more analysis. The most salable kinds of pictures you'll encounter fall into half a dozen groups: scenics (landscapes, seascapes); buildings, skylines, and street scenes; people; animals; inanimate objects (motors, automobiles, and objects of art); and processes (step-by-step pictures showing how something is done).

These groups can be further categorized into shots that are posed and unposed. Many of the pictures you see in magazines that look like candid shots were, in actuality, carefully orchestrated. Perhaps the art director of the magazine you're focusing on goes for group shots of people enjoying some activity. But take unrehearsed pictures of people eating potato salad and you (as well as they) may end up with egg on your face. And shots of the soccer team in action, scattered all over the field, won't win you the points that a seemingly unposed shot of two players confronting each other that you've taken before or after the actual game will.

Excellent photographs frequently sell an editor on a mediocre story because it's simpler for him to improve words than pictures. It follows, therefore, that if you are able to include excellent photos with an excellent story, your chances of a sale will escalate.

According to photographer/writer C.J. Hadley, "It's easy to choose shots to fit a magazine — much easier than writing. Every art director has a quirk and is partial to a certain type of photo, a certain mood. Clip the photos out of the magazine, lay them on the floor and you'll see a personality emerge."

Hadley, whose photos and articles appear in *Saturday Evening Post*, *Autoweek*, *Sports Illustrated*, and other national publications, advises concentrating on verticals because "Most magazine pages are vertical," she says, "and a photo enlarged to page size works better than a horizontal spread across two pages.

"And notice if the art director puts type on photos. Does she like white type on a dark background; black on light? Does he seem to go for print across the middle of a picture, at the bottom or the top? Some magazines have a tendency to use Fuji film and you can tell because the photos are almost always brighter. If they do, use Fuji when you're shooting for them."

Hadley says that you have a better chance of your photos playing bigger (and consequently getting more money for them) if you pay attention to the kinds of shots the art director has demonstrated a preference for. "And," she adds, "always give the art director a couple of options."

Sally Moore, a photographer/writer whose credits include *Innsider*, *Snow Country* and *AAA World*, pays special attention to lighting when she studies a magazine she hasn't supplied material to before, to see if it is bright or subdued. She notes how many establishing shots accompany an article and how many are more specific; if the photos are artsy or calendar-type shots. Moore checks, too, on the ratio of interior to exterior shots used to accompany the kind of article she is submitting, and what types of lenses the photographers have used. "There's a trend for certain magazines to go with more wide-angle shots," she says.

Don Normark, who takes a good many of the photos that appear in *Sunset Magazine*, says that he first "sees what kind of freedom" the magazine lets its photographers have. "The better the magazine, the greater the freedom," he says. Make a list of questions to ask yourself, he advises, such as what sorts of things the editor/art director wants in the shots. And to make efficient use of your time, he recommends that photographers plan what sorts of pictures they are going to shoot and roughly when they are going to shoot them — for example, interior shots at high noon.

My analysis techniques are a combination of hints and tips I've gathered by following professional photographer friends around. I take note of the ratio of horizontal to vertical shots and the size of the pictures, since size has an effect on the kinds of pictures you should submit. As my first photography teacher, Jim Mildon, says, "If a magazine plays pictures very small, you should not send pictures of intricate things; things which cannot be seen in a small space. Many pictures cannot be reduced and still be read."

Some time after taking Mildon's photography course, I attended a workshop conducted by Christopher Springman, who has photographed such diverse subjects as Willie Stargell for *Friends Magazine* and petri dishes for *Smithsonian*.

Springman sees adapting his style to suit the magazine as a challenge. He says he "literally unstaples" six back issues of the publication he's shooting for in order to zero in on its photographic personality. Before he goes out to take the pictures, he has a list — either in his mind or on paper — of the shots he wants to get. "Ninety-five percent of your good shots," he maintains, "don't just happen. They're the result of careful planning."

In addition to giving editors the kinds of shots they've indicated past preferences for, Springman includes photos that incorporate fresh angles (pictures of business executives in the factory with the workers or standing by the company logo in addition to traditional behind-the-desk shots; a check being handed over at the site where the money is to be spent as well as the usual check-presentation shot taken against a plain wall).

Since my specialty is travel writing, I have become especially conscious of the kinds of shots that sell pieces to travel editors. As C.J. Hadley says, they almost always want the scenes in overview or long shots, shots in the middle-range views and close-ups as well.

A nice technique here is the telephoto shot for a magnified slice of the first general shot: details such as a display of produce or crafts in the marketplace, a close-up of the eyes of a Near Eastern beauty, textures of old ruins, grillwork, signs in the local language.

Hadley, Moore, Springman, and other successful freelance photographer/writers have evolved formulas containing many other elements for reading pictures. They look to see whether or not an editor uses captions to carry content that's not in the article. Most magazines use pictures as art in the layout to break up a page or make it graphically attractive. But when the writer/photographer finds that pictures are supposed to carry their own communication, he can adjust his text accordingly. Five paragraphs describing what a rotary engine looks like may not convey the information that a little picture of that engine will, so the writer can briefly describe the engine and let the picture do the rest.

When examining pictures of people, the professional asks herself if the editor goes for posed or unposed shots. She notes whether pictures are taken indoors or out, if they're taken at nighttime or during the day, at dawn or at dusk.

Focusing on Details

You can adapt these techniques of the pros and add some more when planning your pictures. I always pay close attention to the ages of the people in a magazine's pictures, whether they're children, teenagers, adults, senior citizens, or a variety of ages. Then I look to see how they are dressed, casually or in their best clothes. You'll also want to notice if the pictures are head shots, if the subjects are staring at the camera or involved in some activity.

Getting the right kinds of people in your photos is vital. I once took an entire roll of film before I realized that every person in every shot was over the age of sixty-five—not exactly appropriate for the family-oriented magazine I had planned to submit them to. And you'll have better success if you avoid nonphotogenic types. Scruffy looking, obese, or angry-looking people don't have editor appeal when it comes to articles that don't pertain to sloth, overweight, or hostility. Look out for litter, telephone wires and the like, too, unless you're writing about those subjects.

In your picture perusal, determine the amount of action an editor demands. We've all seen publications that feature at least one blurry shot in every issue, connoting speed. Some editors thrive on peak action shots, showing the basketball star jumping with the ball suspended in midair or the cowboy flying off the bronco's back. Other editors go for less vigorous action, such as people walking or knitting or looking through telescopes. There are also those who prefer no action at all—Joshua trees under a desert sun, the reflection of a lake on the mirrored wall of a skyscraper, a castle next to a thatched cottage. While few editors use peak action exclusively or consistently choose static shots, some of them do. What you'll find most often is a mix, but within that mix, a consistent pattern.

A magazine's subject matter dictates in large measure the degree of activity or inactivity its illustrations portray. However (and in analysis, there seem always to be howevers), individual editors see the visual presentation of subject matter through as many different eyes as they do its printed treatment.

To prove this to yourself, examine two magazines that revolve around food and wine, *Gourmet* and *Bon Appétit*. While both magazines use color almost exclusively, most of *Gourmet*'s photos are static shots of various dishes or table settings, whereas those in *Bon Appétit* augment food photos with those of people preparing and eating the featured dishes. There are also more people in the photos accompanying *Bon Appétit*'s food-focused travel pieces than in *Gourmet*'s.

Most editors, whatever their other preferences, like people

to appear in their pictures, whether incidentally or as featured subjects. But there are editors who do not. They prefer their pastures left to the cows, their mountains free of climbers. In almost every picture of a landscape, seascape, or building, though, you'll find some object of recognizable size. Perhaps it's a wildflower or a fire hydrant in the foreground. Editors realize that without this recognizable object there's a problem of scale that makes it impossible to gauge a bluff's height, for example, or whether a valley is ten or one hundred miles wide.

I also try to determine the angles from which an editor likes pictures taken, whether he goes for framing (the ruins seen through an arch or the park bench framed by tree branches), if he seems to like reflections, or any other techniques that give his preferred pictures an unusual quality, a certain something that says, "That picture looks like one from *(blank) Magazine*."

In studying sponsored magazines, I pay special attention to the frequency with which the sponsor's product pops up in pictures illustrating the articles.

You'll find that magazines catering to a specific activity look for photos reinforcing their reason for being. While *Trailer Life* may have a travel trailer or two pictured with an article, don't send trailer photos to *Family Motor Coaching*. Sending them pictures of any kind of recreational vehicle but motor homes says that you haven't read the magazine. Articles in *Golf Digest*, to no one's amazement, are abundantly illustrated with photographs of people playing the game.

When products are present in pictures, it's also important to note whether the brand of that product is obvious or in some way obscured. By reading what's in the pictures (and what is not) you'll be able to establish whether the publication has taboos. You'll see, for example, that *Teens Today* photos feature senior-high-aged boys and girls interacting with people of all ages. But they're pictured differently from the young people in such magazines as *Seventeen* and *Teen*. Since *Teens Today* is published by the Church of the Nazarene, you won't be surprised to find the photography rather conservative, but without studying the pictures closely there's little chance of discovering the less obvious taboos. By examining the photos carefully, you'll see that none of the subjects are dressed in sleeveless clothing, tank tops, body shirts, or shorts. They rarely have jewelry on and the girls never wear earrings. Small details? Unimportant? Not if you want to sell to that market, for the first rule of publishing is "Give 'em what they want."

Who's to Choose?

As you've noticed, we have talked about editors, art directors and designers all being involved in picture decision making at various magazines. At the majority of these publications, each of these people has his or her own ideas about what makes a terrific picture, and either the group defers to the art director, the person with the strongest personality prevails, or the group arrives at a consensus. But the following general criteria should please them all:

1. Good quality (sharp focus; exposure perfect or slightly on the light side since the image tends to get darker when printed; clean, undamaged transparency).

2. The technical requirements must be met, first of all, but strive, too, for artistic merit.

3. Strong composition (dramatic or classic or minimal or busy—something to take it beyond a mere snapshot). The photographer should have attempted to portray something specific—anything from a mood to the lighting to the location of an explicit subject (person, plant, etc.).

4. The photos must relate to the text, usually directly. But they should also add something to the story, such as a mood or a visual detail.

Photo editors' insistence on good quality is not based on whimsy. The process of reproducing a print on paper will cause a marginal print to go to pieces and be unusable. It's all too easy to look at a magazine that's printed on poor quality paper and say, "They'll take any kind of picture. The ones in here are so bad." The photos you scoff at probably were fairly good to begin with; they merely lost a lot in the reproduction. Your best chance of shooting pictures that will reproduce decently on low-grade paper is to take them between ten in the morning and two in the afternoon, at eye level with the sun at your back. It's the standard formula and almost guaranteed to produce usable pictures, though perhaps not the most interesting ones. If the magazine you're shooting for is printed on top-quality paper, you'll be able to go after those pictures that readers want to look at twice — those shot at other times of day and from more exciting angles — without fear that the quality upon reproduction will be compromised.

When you're writing an article about food, you usually won't be expected to supply photos because most magazines have a staff photographer or freelancer who specializes in food photography take them. They do this because photographing food is such a specialized skill — actually a bit like fashion photography — in which the foods to be photographed are shellacked, sprayed, propped up, and arranged just so.

Hollywood-based photographer Peggy Kahana says that celebrity photography is another field the novice can't just "hop into." Kahana, who specializes in taking pictures of celebrities in their homes, advises writers who want to get a start in the field to see if they can take head shots of minor celebrities for public relations firms (perhaps at no pay) and take pictures of friends in their homes so that they can get experience. In deciding on what shots to take, Kahana says the photographer should put herself in the place of the reader and ask, What would I want to see of this person's life?

When You Can't Snap

Even if you do your own photography, there are times when you won't be able to get the pictures you need because of camera catastrophes, rain, and simply not being there. That's when you explore other sources.

Most businesses, chambers of commerce, and other organizations are anxious to have their names before the public. The chance you're offering them — of photo credit and having their product on visual display — spells the kind of publicity that money can't buy, so if they can oblige you, they will. Reading photo credits will give you ideas about people to contact that you hadn't thought of. Going through lists of public agencies, organizations, and industries at the library will provide even more.

Another possible source you'll come upon as you're reading photo credits is other magazines. If they aren't in competition, editors of regional publications especially are willing to have photos from their files printed in other magazines. I was stuck for photos to go with an article I did on the Elko, Nevada, Basque Festival. My logical source was the Basque Studies Institute at the University of Nevada-Reno. The only suitable pictures they had were a group that had been taken by *Sunset Magazine*. I was given the shots with the stipulation that the editor of the magazine in which my piece was to appear must get *Sunset*'s permission before using any of them. Next, since my intended publication also uses color and the *Sunset* photos were black and white, I approached *Nevada Magazine*, a publication sponsored by the state department of economic development. They turned me loose on their photo file, and I was able to choose the other pictures I needed.

You'll find that you must be selective in choosing the source photos that you plan to submit. Many pictures of products put out by their manufacturers are unsuitable for your purposes. For example, I once needed color slides of motorcycles for a piece I was writing for a European magazine. Most of those I got were cheesecake shots with scantily clad beauties sitting behind the handlebars, so I ended up going to showrooms, persuading the personnel to move the bikes into more photogenic positions and taking the shots myself.

Many tourism department travel photos are too much like advertising art to work for travel articles — the hotel room interior, the obviously posed donkey cart ride, the couple frolicking in the surf. And all too often, the black-and-white photos haven't enough contrast, while the color slides are fourth- or fifth-generation dupes (duplicates) that won't reproduce properly.

When asking for photos, be specific about what you need. Be frank about the necessity for good quality photos and you'll cut down on the number of useless pictures you receive.

When several photographers are given photo credits in the same article, there is no sure way to tell whether those photos were supplied by freebie sources or obtained from stock photo agencies, or who did the scrambling to get them together, the editorial staff or the freelancer. I've found that when I can't get free photos, it's better to let an editor know that pictures are available from big stock photo agencies than to procure them myself. The first reason is economic. Fees at most agencies start at around twenty-five dollars for a one-time use of a black-and-white picture and can run as high as hundreds of dollars for some color transparencies. Unless the writer's payment for photos from the magazine will amount to more than these charges, obtaining them is unprofitable and time-consuming. Some agencies set their rates in accordance with the publication in which the pictures will appear, so the writer can't be sure there will be a margin of profit.

There can also be additional costs in the form of research fees. These are refundable or deducted from the total bill after a magazine makes its selection. But if none of the photos are chosen, there is a possibility that whoever contracted for them will be stuck with paying the research fee. A penalty charge for keeping the pictures longer than a specified period makes the use of these pictures impractical, too, when you're submitting an article on spec or one for which a publication date has not been set.

And there's still another pitfall. I desperately needed transparencies for an article and telephoned a stock photo agency to inquire about available photos and charges, then asked them to send a selection of forty slides. When they arrived, I read the fine print on the use agreement and found to my horror that in case they were lost or damaged I would have to pay fifteen hundred dollars for each of the originals and a smaller sum for each duplicate. Since almost all of the transparencies were originals, my total liability could have amounted to about sixty-five thousand dollars. Needless to say, I immediately rebundled the package and drove very carefully to the post office to send it back registered and insured. I had to pay the research fee, but twenty dollars was a small price for the lesson I learned.

Editors across the board say that just as they're negatively impressed by messy manuscripts, they're put off by the unprofessional photo presentation of many freelancers. Slides should be properly placed in plastic sleeves (sheets that hold twenty 35mm color transparencies cost less than fifty cents at most camera stores) so that all the backs are facing the same way and verticals are placed vertically so that the whole page can be viewed at a glance. Needless to say, every shot you submit should be in focus and properly exposed.

Studying all the pictures in the magazine isn't only profitable, it's fun. And when you're submitting photos on the basis of what you have learned, remember to include some vertical shots with light space at the top for the magazine's logo. After all, if you've done your homework well, one of your pictures could wind up on the cover.

When you receive photos from tourist bureaus, manufacturers and other sources, be sure to return the pictures when the magazine has finished using them.

Be sure that any tourist bureau photos, especially, are up-to-date before you send them along with the manuscript to your targeted magazine. You would be amazed at how old some of the shots are — the British Tourist Authority, for instance, has photos in its files dating back to 1971.

Chapter Five

Your Style Is My Style

Every style that is not boring is a good one.

Voltaire

*A*ll the fun's in how you say a thing," Robert Frost once wrote. And saying a thing in the way an editor likes it said makes it even more fun as far as I'm concerned, because I love to fill out those deposit slips at the bank.

How you say a thing is actually a good definition of style — the ingredient that goes a long way in tempting editorial palates. It's the quality that gives distinction to writing, one of the means whereby a magazine develops that flavor its editor is eager to perpetuate. But since editors' tastes are so diverse, it is essential that you analyze what they've bought in the past to determine how you should serve it up in the future. You'll find that some editors like large helpings of folksy chatter. Others prefer their copy sprinkled with sophistication. Still others want theirs straight, with no garnishes.

You may have your subject matter down cold. Your grammar and spelling may be above reproach; your title, terrific; your manuscript, unsmudged. The idea may fit its intended publication like a wetsuit. But if you haven't written that article to the editor's stylistic appetite, be doubly sure there's enough postage on that SASE.

The successful freelancer is a writing chameleon. He

blends at will with the surrounding editorial pages of whatever magazine he's writing for at the moment, changing the coloration of his prose as he moves from piece to piece. There are a few writers who are able to live handsomely by specializing in one field and writing for only a handful of top-paying slicks. The operative word here is *few*. Most of us, in order to subsist at above-poverty level, must be able not only to write about a variety of subjects, but also to pull, push, and pummel our writing styles about like chunks of Play-doh. It stands to reason that the greater number of publications we're able to write for, the more chances we have of seeing those five fascinating words, "Pay to the order of."

This verbal blending allows you to write in a breezy, freewheeling way one day, with authoritative, no-nonsense sentences the next. It's not difficult to emulate a certain style if you've done your analysis homework. After all, you don't talk about the same things or in the same manner to your best friend as you do to your father-in-law, your children, or the newsboy on the corner. When you have a clear picture of a magazine's readership, of the working of its editor's mind (at least during business hours), and the kinds of articles she has gone for in the past, style transformations become automatic. Look at these excerpts from articles in three publications and you'll see what I mean.

Professor William Steed, DFP, is an original—a combination educator, favorite uncle and flimflam man. Although he has been likened to both Will Rogers and Harpo Marx, there's a sprinkling of Professor Harold Hill, Captain Kangaroo and the Wizard of Oz thrown in just for good measure. For when the professor puts on his top hat and frock coat to talk about Croaker College, you can't help wondering if what he says is on the level or if he's spinning you the greatest yarn ever told.

Professor Steed, DFP, is dean of the world's only institute of higher learning for frogs. And if you haven't already heard, Steed's school has gained a worldwide reputation for producing champion calibre jumping frogs. To clarify the importance of his stature, the letters after Professor Steed's name stand for Doctor of Frog Psychology.

That article, called "Jumpin' Jehosophat!" appeared in an airline in-flight magazine. The next one was printed in a business publication.

Nevada banks are betting a change in that state's laws will enable them to get a piece of the biggest gambling pie—slot machines.

Assembly Bill 211, passed by the Nevada State Legislature in its 1977 session, allows banks or bank subsidiaries based in the state to lease gaming equipment without obtaining a gaming license. Before the law's passage, banks were allowed to make loans on all kinds of gaming equipment and lease such gambling devices as 21 tables and Keno equipment, but were prohibited from leasing slot machines, backbone of the state's multimillion-dollar gaming industry.

The third example is part of an article that appeared in a women's magazine.

We're all battling to make our food budgets stretch as far as possible these days. But many homemakers don't realize that their freezers (and refrigerator freezing compartments) can be their staunchest allies in the struggle against rising prices. A well-managed freezer means food economy as well as better meals. Bargain strawberries tucked away in June taste twice as tempting in December. Chicken Parmesan prepared on a day when you're not busy can be a money-saving work-saver on a day when you are. All it takes to enlist the aid of your freezer is a bit of planning on your part.

As you can see, the first example is written in a carefree, relaxed style. The second is reportorial, and the third is written in an instructional manner that sounds like a home economist talking to a group of homemakers. I wrote all three articles within a few weeks' time. But they were written about different subjects, for different audiences, and most important, for different editors. By studying the magazines, I found it was easy to adapt my style to their individual tastes. Without that analysis, the job would have been far more difficult.

Though it's possible to adapt your style to hundreds of publications, don't be dismayed if you can't become a man for all magazines. Few writers can. You will find that there are some you simply cannot write for—but often, not for the reasons you would imagine.

Once upon a time, I queried a magazine without ever having seen it. When the editor replied with a go-ahead on speculation, I started gathering back issues, something I should have done in the beginning. Each time I'd try to read the articles that the editor presumably had thought interesting, I would find it impossible to concentrate. Though many of the subjects were compelling, the writing was extremely stiff and inordinately dull. I wouldn't do that to *my* exciting topic. So I wrote the piece in a style I liked. Needless to say, my brown manila came back to me with a stiff, dull note saying that unfortunately it wouldn't fit the publication.

It's also difficult to write for a magazine whose subject matter doesn't interest you or is well beyond your experience level. You're not going to be able to do a satisfactory piece of contemporary political satire if, like me, you have trouble understanding "Doonesbury." If searching out the sidewalk café where it's ultimate status to sip an aperitif isn't your scene, you'll probably have difficulty coping with the style of articles appealing to travelers in search of snob appeal.

An occasional editor has a penchant for complicated words. Whether or not you're a wizard with complex language will determine your ability to produce copy for the ultraliterates. But even if your everyday conversation isn't peppered with polysyllables, you'll find that you and your trusty thesaurus are better able than you think to write for magazines whose editors prefer a Bill Buckley vocabulary.

Often when you find yourself incapable of imitating a magazine's style, the reason isn't your inability to write. It's because you don't have enough material that lends itself to that particular way of telling the story. Perhaps you are short on anecdotes or don't have enough facts. You may have neglected to obtain the kind of information the editor likes writers to use in their leads; it might be that you need more authoritative-sounding quotes. I've found that impossible-to-write pieces almost fell out of the typewriter once I'd collected the missing parts.

Elementary Elements of Style

Read a variety of articles to find styles compatible with your writing. Which do you find most interesting and enjoyable to read? Chances are, it will be easier for you to write in those styles, too.

But before you begin analyzing the styles of individual articles, it's a good idea to analyze the components of style itself. They are tone, point of view, sentence length and type, descriptive words, reading level, kind of verbs, and personality devices.

Setting the Tone

Tone determines whether a piece will be academic, formal, straightforward, instructional, reportorial, lighthearted, or humorous. To say that subject matter dictates tone in many cases is true, but it can also be an oversimplification. Take houseplants, for example. Scholarly botanical journals require formally written, technically complex articles about them. General interest magazines will usually go for a conversational, less technical approach, while houseplant articles in magazines devoted to house and garden generally fall somewhere in between. While most pieces on the subject are of the serious, informational variety, it's possible to treat the topic with a light touch, even with humor, or with a negative rather than a positive slant—"To Hell with Houseplants" or "I'm Splitting with My Philodendron."

Tone is established primarily by the language used: formal, informal or colloquial. Formal language is textbook English, the kind you were supposed to use in high school compositions. Pronouns and auxiliary verbs are always written in full. Slang or trendy phrases are never used, except as a point of discussion, and then they're enclosed by quotation marks. Punctuation, complete with colons and semicolons, is used according to standard rules.

Informal writing is far more relaxed, and most editors today prefer it for conversational rapport between writer and readers. Strangely enough (since we've all been talking in a casual manner for years), writing informally is a problem with most beginning writers. Even those of us with more experience have trouble occasionally with stilted writing. Whenever I feel my style needs relaxing, I tell the story I'm trying to write to my tape recorder. By pretending it's a conversation with a friend, I can make the ghosts from my English-theme-writing days disappear, and the narrative flows.

There are other tricks you will learn from the magazines you're studying. Use contractions. *He's* reads more informally than *he is*, *they're* rolls off the eye less stiffly than *they are*. The first person and second person techniques have been adopted by many editors not only for reader identification, but also for their more informal style. You'll find, too, that some editors don't object to a sentence fragment now and then, if the meaning is clear to the reader. Stream-of-consciousness writing generally doesn't work, though, because associations have to be clear to everyone reading a piece, not just to the few whose consciousness streams in the same channels as the writer's.

Another technique involves throwing in an aside now and then or using parenthetical material. Punctuation, which dictates the way material is read, also goes a long way toward informalizing style. Somehow, a parenthetical expression set off by dashes becomes less formal than if commas are used. Colons and semicolons stiffen the tone. In colloquial writing, quotation marks or italics are seldom used to set the down-home phrases apart; words are allowed to flow visually unimpeded.

Colloquial writing incorporates words and phrases that have become a part of language because of their use in everyday speech. These words and phrases may defy all the rules of grammar—ain't, have gotten—but some editors see them as part of their magazines' images. We tend to think of colloquial writing in terms and phrases from bygone eras or such regions of the country as the Deep South or the Ozarks. Colloquial to us means *younguns, y'all come, folk*. But there are contemporary colloquialisms as well. People often *rap* instead of talk in *Sassy* articles; boys are called *guys*, and pimples, *zits*. *Essence* writers refer to other blacks as *brothers* and *sisters*. Pick up a copy of magazines like *Rolling Stone* and *Easyriders* and you'll see contemporary colloquialisms that you had better become familiar with if you want to write for those publications.

When you use colloquialisms, pay special attention to how

they have been treated in past issues. Although most editors look upon the enclosure of colloquial phrases in quotation marks as an affectation, some of them do use quotation marks, while others italicize the words.

It is difficult to capture colloquial speech, so difficult in fact that many authorities on writing argue against trying. But since there are editors who like their articles flavored with the vernacular of an area or group of people, the writer who wants to sell must go counter to the experts' advice, proceeding with care and caution so as not to sound patronizing.

There's also a nonmechanical component that enters into the tone-altering process, one by which the writer gains a feel for the mood and tone he or she wants to produce. I've found that writers have a variety of gimmicks for changing their inner voices, many of which involve role-playing. When I'm writing a straight news story, for example, I picture myself as a sort of nonabrasive Barbara Walters. From first interview to final paragraph I'm all business, and while writing I sit at my computer, notes in organized piles on the desk.

By contrast, when I'm writing a "you are there" travel piece, I flop on the sofa, listen to music of the country I'm writing about, and look at pictures of the places I want to re-create for my readers. Not long ago I met a writer who, whenever he wants to do a freewheeling, relaxed piece, takes to his bathtub (with notepad, pencil, *and* boats). Whatever props and fantasies work for you, use them.

How do you judge what tone to use? By analyzing previously published pieces on parallel themes, by developing a feeling for what is appropriate to the particular magazine, by becoming sensitive to the publication's readership. Words and phrases like "of course," "obviously," and "as you know" may work in an article for one magazine and sound condescending in another. A flip approach to a serious subject can be the answer to an editor's prayers, or anathema. What's considered good taste varies tremendously between publications.

You'll find that tone, in general, has changed significantly during the past decade. The conversational approach, which entertains as it imparts information, continues to become more popular each year. Words haven't become shorter or easier, necessarily, but the way they're strung together has.

For instance, ten years ago an article on moving up the corporate ladder would most probably have sounded like a how-to lecture, with examples thrown in here and there to illustrate various points. By contrast, today's article on the same subject will more likely read like a series of stories interspersed with informational amplification.

In combating the competition from TV's painless presentations, magazine editors search for articles to so engross readers that they don't necessarily turn the pages for information, but rather because they want to see how everything turns out in the end, be it someone's lovelife or their skin rejuvenation regimen.

Whatever tone you adopt, be aware that certain words that were "in" last decade are now definitely "out." Consider *ubiquitous* and *halcyon*. Although those words have been around since the days of Daniel Webster, their overusage in the 1980s made them seem as if they had been born in that decade.

By contrast, *clearly* is an early-1990s word if you ever heard one. Rarely spoken in the 1980s, during those years people were more likely to say *it's clear that* or *obviously*.

I, You or They

Another element that determines style is *point of view*. You'll notice that while most articles are written in the third person, there is a growing trend toward first-person accounts. The former is standard in informational articles, especially those about technical or semitechnical subjects, and in personality pieces. First person, though very much in vogue during the nineteenth century and first few decades of the twentieth, was out of favor until recent years. Now first-person accounts are back in editorial fashion, but are unlike those of times past, which sounded like pages from diaries.

Careful study of published articles will show you how to craft your first-person accounts. They usually begin with first person, then after a paragraph or two slip into third, catching up the first-person thread at intervals throughout the piece. How often that thread is caught up will come to light as you read first-person articles in varied publications. Another secret of successful first-person writing is to avoid straight chronology, except in a few publications that go for personalized, blow-by-blow recapitulations of experiences. Even then, you will notice that the articles don't recount every detail of the experience. In travel articles, for example, brushing your teeth and parking the car aren't mentioned unless they're relevant (*How to Write and Sell Your Personal Experiences* by Lois Duncan will give you lots of good information on this type of piece.) Second person is the predominant form of address in how-to articles, especially those that explain projects. There, the imperative form of the verb (Measure three inches; Glue the corners; Solder wire A to terminal B) is used. Second person is also combined with first and third in pieces whose purpose is to rouse the reader to action (Write your congressman; You can help by . . . .) or to acquaint him with a place, event or pastime (You'll find that . . . . ; Across the river you'll see . . . . ; And don't miss the . . . .).

The point of view you choose can have a direct impact on your sales success. Editors who always buy third-person articles almost never consider others, and editors who print only first-person pieces won't look twice at those done in second or third no matter how well they're written.

Give 'em the (Right) Word

The nouns you use are important, but you'll realize as you read articles analytically that it's the adjectives that set the outstanding pieces apart. The quantity of *descriptive words* used in an article does much to establish its style, and the number of them that different editors like varies widely. Be on the alert for adverbs, too, and notice the changes they make in how an article sounds.

You will find in your reading that most editors prefer active *verbs*. They give an article zing, while the passive voice makes it drag. But there's a great deal of difference among active verbs. In some magazines they are definitely punchy; in others they seem to be there only as a necessary part of each sentence. If an editor has shown a preference for such powerful verbs as *ricocheted*, *sizzled*, and *careened*, he's sure to want equally colorful ones in the future. And speaking of future, note what tense the editor prefers. Usually you'll see that it's a combination, but you will find magazines in which almost all verbs are in present tense. (There's a wonderfully helpful discussion of active and passive voice in *The Careful Writer* by Theodore Bernstein.)

One emerging trend the careful analyst will note is that of using not only active verbs, but those in the present tense. A technique used by novelists to give readers a sense of participation, this active verb style is usually used in nonfiction that's written in the first person.

Beware the Fog

Since editors are aware of the average educational level of their readerships, they are careful not to print material those readers might have difficulty comprehending. In fact, they work to make reading both easy and enjoyable. Zeroing in on the readability of a particular publication is one of the easiest jobs in analysis.

For some thirty-five years, the late Robert Gunning overhauled the prose of more than two hundred publications, including the *Wall Street Journal*. In the process he invented the "fog index," a way to compute the years of schooling needed to understand a piece of writing. By using this index you can analyze various pieces in your target publication and see whether your article's readability corresponds. Here's how you use this handy formula:

1. Find the average number of words per sentence in a sample of one or two hundred words. Treat clearly independent clauses as separate sentences.

2. Figure the percentage of words having three or more syllables. Don't count capitalized words, easy combinations like "lawnmower," or verbs that have three syllables because of the addition of *-es* or *-ed*.

3. Add the average sentence length to the percentage of big words. Multiply the total by 0.4. The number that results indicates the years of schooling needed to understand the piece.

4. Repeat the process for several samples in various parts of the article and average the results.

As a rule, as the circulation size of a magazine increases, the fog index goes down. *TV Guide* has a fog index of six. The *Wall Street Journal*, *Time* and *Newsweek* average about eleven.

Superstructure your sentences. We've all read that the writer should vary *sentence length* and *type*. Generally, that holds true. But while some editors have a passion for forty-word sentences, others prefer an almost staccato style. There's variation in length, all right, but that variation may be between thirty-five and sixty words, or between four and eight. As a rule, the average sentence is shorter in large-circulation magazines than in those with smaller circulations, since widely read publications aim for reading ease.

You'll find definite editorial preferences as far as sentence type is concerned, too. In your analysis you will encounter not only the three basic structures—simple, compound and complex—but a host of different sentence patterns as well. The twenty-five most common ways to begin a sentence follow as an example of construction diversity:

1. Noun-verb:
   Winter arrives early in Finland.
2. Personal pronoun-verb:
   He ran from the burning vehicle.
3. Inverted verb:
   Perched atop the archway were two bronze cherubs.
4. Prepositional phrase:
   At the top of the pile was a sealed document.
5. Adjective:
   Large profits can be expected in the next two years.
6. Adverb:
   Steadily the waters advanced toward the campsite.
7. Adverbial phrase:
   Ahead of time, make arrangements to ship the merchandise.
8. Adverbial clause:
   When the water has begun to boil, add the noodles.

9. Coordinating conjunction:
   Nor does the broom do as thorough a job as the vacuum cleaner.

10. Direct object:
    Tacks you can store in a small container.

11. Indefinite pronoun:
    Such is the case when a new travel destination becomes popular.

12. Series:
    Date, hour and meeting place were decided upon.

13. Participial phrase:
    Reaching your goal, you may want to celebrate.

14. Participle:
    Baked, the cake looks very much like brownies.

15. Gerund:
    Jogging can become addictive.

16. Gerund phrase:
    Running long distances should be done during the cool part of the day.

17. Infinitive:
    To win, a player must score the most points.

18. Infinitive phrase:
    To pay by credit card has become the accepted form of business.

19. Noun clause:
    That you may learn Spanish in ten days is not as impossible as you think.

20. Imperative:
    Take as much time as you need.

21. Connective:
    However, the decreasing availability of fuel may cause rising prices.

22. Transitional phrase:
    By the same token, they are generous with their possessions.

23. Appositive:
    An acknowledged expert in his field, the curator is on hand to answer visitors' questions.

24. Adverb of question:
    Where can you find the proper instruction?

25. Absolute phrase:
    The forms placed in their positions, you can begin mixing the cement.

These types of beginnings are only starters in the sentence-patterning game. If you really want to delve into the subject, consult *American English Rhetoric* by E.G. Bander, which you can find at most libraries. Another classic, the favorite of many freelancers, is Strunk and White's *The Elements of Style*. Whether you read these books or not, you should learn to recognize the different types of sentences. Most often, you will find a variety of types in an article. You'll rarely see a series of sentences that involves mechanical symmetry, for several compound sentences in a row, all with the same conjunction, become boring. For the same reason, sentences beginning with phrases don't often follow one after the other.

House Rules

There's a second meaning of style that writers should know about. It's what is referred to by publishers as *house style* or *press style* and involves the rules regarding the mechanics of written communication—spelling, punctuation, capitalization and the like (we'll talk more about punctuation in chapter eight). Editors commonly use style as a verb in the context that styling a manuscript means to fix the capitalization, hyphenation, and spelling in conformity with house rules.

Most editors don't expect writers to be completely aware of their publications' mechanical styles, but it *is* important to prepare your manuscripts in conformity to some sort of style (the University of Chicago Press's *The Chicago Manual of Style* and the *Associated Press Stylebook* are two excellent references). If you can zero in on a particular editor's mechanical style preferences, however, you'll have tallied up another plus.

Personality Producers

The preceding elements of style are largely mechanical. The final element, *personality devices*, gives an article soul. Some kinds of pieces, granted, don't lend themselves to artistic expression. But if zestful writing is a feature of the magazine you wish to sell to, yours had better be just as lively. Personality devices include quotes, anecdotes, figures of speech, and sometimes the descriptive words mentioned earlier in the chapter. When you're analyzing a magazine, notice not only the sort of quotes that are used, but also their length, their source, and their tone (humorous, instructional, startling). Note also the function of these quotes. Are they used to lighten the piece, to add credibility, to increase the human interest quality?

An anecdote, according to Webster, is "a narrative, usually brief, of a separable incident or event of curious interest, often biographical." In simpler language, it is a short story that serves to amplify, a device many editors like used in liberal doses, but others ignore. While you're on the lookout for quotes in an article, notice anecdotes, using the same guidelines to determine what kind an editor likes. You'll find that some of them are everyday "slices of life"; others recapitulate important events. They range from a few sentences to several paragraphs in length.

When you're reading, be conscious of any *figures of speech* the writers have used. In case you've repressed memories of high school English classes in which you had to write ten examples each of *metaphors*, *similes* and *personification*, here's a quickie refresher course.

A *simile* is a figure of speech by which one thing, action or relation is likened or explicitly compared, often using *as* or *like*, to something of a different kind or quality. (I remember what similes are by recalling the line from "Oh, What a Beautiful Mornin' " about the corn being as high as an elephant's eye.)

Metaphor is the use of a word or phrase denoting one object or idea in the place of another to suggest a likeness or analogy between them — the ship plows the sea; a volley of oaths.

Personification is attribution of personal form, character and the like to an inanimate object or abstract idea as endowed with personal attributes — the city opens its arms; the country-side, dressed for spring.

Some words of warning: Though figures of speech can be exceedingly effective, they won't bring any editorial plaudits when they're not done well. Be sure that your similes are apt *and* fresh, that your personifications are within the realm of your readers' imaginations. Beware of clumsy or mixed metaphors.

Concocting the Formula

After you have studied several articles in a publication, you will be able to mix together the proper proportions of stylistic ingredients for your own piece. If the content of your article lends itself to two or three different styles the editor seems to like, go with the one that will result in the greatest reader arousal.

A study in the late 1970s by the University of Kentucky Department of Communications showed that readers react more positively to the narrative story with strong descriptive adjectives and verbs than to any other. If that study were conducted today, the results would undoubtedly show that the narrative story is even more popular now.

Readers also express preferences for pieces containing direct quotes rather than paraphrased statements. Above all, when there's a choice to be made, rely on your writer's sense.

One thing is certain. Whatever style you adopt for a particular article, you cannot afford to ignore the elements of good writing. Just because an editor likes fifty-six word sentences doesn't mean that your modifiers can dangle or that you're free to disregard punctuation. Singular verbs with plural nouns (strata, phenomena, media, and data seem to cause the most problems) won't do the job even if your article is loaded with the kind of picturesque writing the editor adores.

Remember that a sentence expresses a complete thought. Even though some of your potential buyers show a tolerance for sentence fragments, those incomplete sentences have to make sense. Otherwise, they will appear to be syntactical or punctuation blunders. And be sure to say exactly what you mean. I once edited a report about a program that enabled teenaged mothers to continue in high school while their babies were cared for in a nursery. The writer, trying to explain the program, said, "The girls are able to continue with their education while their babies are cared for until they have graduated from high school."

Use definite, specific language. Avoid superfluous words. Pay special attention to adjectives. Are they the most effective, descriptive modifiers you can use? Avoid clichés and overworked words, but take care in coining your own words and phrases. Even if the editor seems to buy articles full of newly minted expressions, yours can't be obscure or inappropriate. Orthodox spelling (night, not nite; through, not thru) is important, too, unless you are writing for the rare editor who prefers the shortened forms.

With a little bit of help from my editor friends, I've collected the following excerpts from articles that fall into the "least likely to see publication" category:

"As a mother of six, and pregnant to boot, my washing machine is always full."

"Salads, tossed, cut or wilted are the byword this year by the diet the customers at the _____ Hotel are no exception."

"Striking women three times more often than men, its victims are primarily the young adult in the prime of life."

"A senior citizen that I talked to recently recounted to me the reason . . . ."

"Get up in the morning, look out the window and see the sun rise. And if you don't, it will probably be overcast."

"Relevant to the current mania for computer games, I have made a study into the subject."

Though you can learn from bad examples, you'll profit more by studying the successes. Fortunately for the freelancer, they're easy to find. Just reach for the nearest magazine.

Chapter Six

The Name Game

A good name is better than precious ointment.

Ecclesiastes

*I*n the prologue of John Steinbeck's novel *Sweet Thursday*, his Cannery Row character, Mac, suggests that the author insert a little hooptedoodle in his book now and then. Hooptedoodle, according to Mac, is some pretty words, maybe, or a little song sung with language—not part of the book, really, but an insert.

I agree with Mac. Every book should have a bit of hooptedoodle, a little something that allows the reader to relax and wiggle his mind. So let's hooptedoodle it up right now with a game.

Titling for Style and Impact

The following fifteen titles appeared in three magazines. Your challenge is to decide which five go together and were published in the same magazine. The answers are on the next page, but you won't need to peek.

1. IRS leaves Willie Nelson homeless and broke
2. Bowl Game Buffet
3. Jack-O-Lantern Jamboree
4. Dan Rather keeps me off CBS news, claims bitter Cronkite

5. Joyful Barbara Eden weds for the 3rd time
6. Exploring the Sutter Buttes
7. Discovering the Scenic East Mojave
8. Fabulous Fall Desserts
9. 'Guns N'Roses' star brutally beaten in barroom brawl
10. Riding the "Short Lines"
11. Terrific Turkey Entrees
12. Fudge Made Fast
13. Lovesick Mike Tyson under suicide watch
14. Exploring Shasta County
15. Bracing for the Big One

You're right! Titles 1, 4, 5, 9, and 13 go together. They appeared in *National Enquirer*. Titles 2, 3, 8, 11, and 12 were in *Bon Appétit*; 6, 7, 10, 14, and 15 appeared in *Motorland*. I could have substituted heads from hundreds of magazines and the game would have been just as simple to play. Editors are incredibly consistent in their title choices, a fact avid article analysts can use to good advantage.

Why bother? Titles aren't that important, you contend. Editors always change them. Wait a minute. They don't *always*. If your title is compatible with the publication's personality, fits the layout, and the editor can't come up with one she likes better, she'll use it. Even if the title is changed, you score points by coming up with a good one — good, in this case, meaning one appropriate to the publication. And add another plus for *perfect* titles. Editors, like readers, can be hooked by them. A title that catches the editor's imagination will make her want to like the piece, make her visualize the title printed in her magazine.

If you can devise a just-right title at the time you're querying, your chances of a sale escalate. An editor who hasn't worked with you before has no evidence of your ability. It's difficult for him to decide whether to take a chance that you're reliable, that you'll deliver an article suited to his magazine. Upon first glance at your custom-designed title, he'll see you're on his frequency, and that's the best of all editor-writer beginnings.

In the course of your analysis, you'll see that titles (or heads or headlines, as they're sometimes called) fall into four major categories: label, imperative, interrogative, and statement. Use the following definitions and examples as a guide to identifying them.

The Label

I can't count the number of times I've read that label titles are somehow second-rate, last resorts to be avoided. Be that as it may, editors choose labels for their pieces more often than others. The label can consist of only a noun ("Honey"), a noun with modifiers ("Greek Getaway"; "Male Angst") or include verbs ("Traveling on Business with Children"; "Breaking Up without Breaking Down"). When a verb is included, it's usually in the present progressive tense as in the preceding examples, but it doesn't have to be ("How to Keep Your Man Happy in Bed"; "We Love a Parade").

Imperative

Another favorite is the *imperative*. It's a stronger title than the rather passive label in that it urges the reader to action ("Let the Kids Know You Love Them"; "Don't Put Today's Pleasures Off Until Tomorrow"). Imperatives are often used to title how-to pieces such as "Cut Out Cholesterol" and "Win the Entertaining Game."

Interrogative

Editors who like the *interrogative* title believe that by asking a question, they elicit reader response to the article before it's even read. Titles like "What's with All the Asian-Bashing?" "Who's Polluting America?" and "Puzzled by Health Insurance?" can hook a reader even if she's casually flipping through the magazine.

Statement

The *statement* title is exactly that, a short sentence stating the theme of the article, such as "The Post-Gringo Era Begins in Central America" and "Playing with Blocks Can Be a Fine Art at this Theme Park" (about Mt. Rushmore).

Often two title types, or two of the same type, are combined in what I call the *two-parter*. It's a cinch to recognize because it always contains either a colon or a dash—"Dallas: D is for Diversity"; "Sex Appeal—Subtle Ways to Catch His Eye." Although both parts of a two-parter are usually labels, they can also incorporate the interrogative, imperative, or statement. Actually, the two-parter is much like the label title/blurb combination. The words before the colon or dash (usually one to four of them) name or describe the article's subject. The words following the punctuation summarize the article's slant.

Although most titles fall into these four groups, there's wide variation in the devices used to construct them. You'll notice that articles' names are often alliterative, most of their words beginning with the same sound—"Tacos, Tackles and Touchdowns," "The Rage for Roots," "6 Ways to Earn Power, Prestige, Perks and a Promotion." *Travel & Leisure* editors employed alliteration to an extreme in "Simply Super Shopping" followed by the blurb "From Harrods to Hyper."

Another device is the play on words. Some editors go overboard with these plays on words and phrases; others shun them entirely. One magazine that uses a lot of them is *Mirabella*, with such titles as "Finn de Siecle" (a story about Finnish film-maker Aki Kaurismaki), "Ertha Watch" (profiling the provisional president of Haiti, Ertha Pascal-Trouillot), and "Hot as a Pistil" (about a collection of Robert Mapplethorpe's flower portraits).

Several years ago, *Smithsonian* ran a story about a nineteenth-century paleontologist who had willed his body to his university. A present-day faculty member later discovered the old fellow's skeleton in storage. Thinking a storage room not a fit resting place for a distinguished man of science, the professor took the bones and gave them a place of honor in his office. He decorated them with tinsel at Christmas and drank toasts to old Dr. So-and-So's memory. The title was "Not Alive, but Well."

Popular vehicles for wordplay and parody are well-known slogans, TV shows, book titles, and quotes or words from a song or poem. "From Here to Maternity" in *Entrepreneurial Woman* told about the designer of clothes for pregnant career women. "Suture Shock" in *Mirabella* talked about plastic surgery and its excesses; "Future Choc" in *Chocolatier* involved predictions about chocolate consumption in the years ahead. A piece in *Compass* called "Wheels of Fortune" was followed by the blurb "Napa Valley on a Ten Speed." "Kitsch and Tell" in *Harper's Bazaar* titled an article about two Parisian pop iconographers.

Another wordplay title I like is "Looking for Mr. Goldbar," which headed an article on finding a rich husband in *American Woman*. "The Prattle of the Sexes," "Get Up and Glow" (on aerobics), "A Touch-Up of Class" (on hair coloring) and "What's Updike?" are other effective wordplay/parody titles.

You'll notice that most titles of this type can stand by themselves, a fact important to keep in mind when you're constructing a wordplay/parody title.

Those of us in the age group my ex-hairdresser refers to as elderly (over forty-five) must take care that the phrases we think everyone's familiar with really *are* widely known.

It's fine to parody a pre-World War II song title if you're writing for a nostalgia publication or one whose audience is in the fifty-plus age group, but chances are teens and young adults won't appreciate your efforts. By the same token, young writers, when putting together articles for an audience encompassing all age groups, will leave many of their readers mystified if they base titles on recent rock hits.

Another title-making trick is to rhyme words: "The Blame Game" (a piece on the art of avoiding accountability), "Cape Escape" (about vacationing on Cape Cod), and "May Day is Lei Day" (about the statewide holiday in Hawaii).

Using a word or phrase that has a different meaning when spelled differently can also be effective if it's done well. Among those I've thought especially clever were "Bone Appetit: Rating Pet Foods," "Ciao Down," a story about Italian restaurant dining, and "A Traveler's Tail . . . Vacationing with Your Pet." As you can see, in order for them to work, there must be an association between the phrase you've taken off on and the article's subject.

Coining a word, such as "Habersplashery" (a fashion article in *Esquire* several years ago), or playing off a better-known aspect of a place, are two other techniques. A good example of the latter was "The Other Tables of Las Vegas," a label title for an article on dining out that was printed in *Bon Appétit*.

Although on occasion you may find a sensational headline

in a general interest magazine, they're generally used only in tabloids and detective magazines. I've never sold an article with a sensational title, but I love reading the more outrageous ones. Pick up any issue of *Star*, *Globe* or *National Examiner*, and you'll find titles like "Poodle Whips a Pit Bull to Save Two-year-old Girl," "Hubby Dumps Wife Who Won't Stop Cleaning Up," "Baked Bean Bath Cures Arthritis," and "Scientists Vanish after UFO Sighted on Mount Everest."

First cousin to the sensational title is the shocker/terrifier. You'll usually find this type in general circulation magazines — "Where Will Terrorists Strike Next?" "Are We Headed for Armageddon?"

Paradox is popular, too, and not difficult to construct. "Be a Big Spender on a Budget" and "Win by Losing" are effective titles born of contrast. "Down East Up Close," "Little League's Mr. Big," and "Not-So-Easy-Riders" (about exercise bikes) achieve their effects by relying on words that are in opposition or that are unexpected given the context.

Finally, you can give words or phrases a meaning other than that usually associated with them. One of the best titles created by this device that I've read was in *Friends*. It was "Water Colors," followed by the blurb "Mix Key Largo's neon-bright sea life with Key Biscayne's island pastels and hot Hispanic reds for a trip through a tropical palette."

Double entendre — using a phrase that has a double meaning, one of them usually indelicate — is tricky. Although a few publications thrive on sexual innuendo, profanity, and four-letter words, most magazines consider that kind of writing taboo.

Actually, other than blue language, most anything goes in titles. You *will* want to take care, however, that your title doesn't either put the reader down or scold him.

Title Tailoring Tricks

Once you know what kinds of titles an editor likes, there are several tricks you can use to come up with just what she wants. First, examine your capsule sentence to see if it can be paraphrased and shortened. Consult your thesaurus for synonyms.

If you're searching for an imperative title, ask yourself what you are trying to get the reader to do. Then start your urge to action with a verb you know the editor goes for. Strange though it may seem, certain words are repeated over and over again in magazines during the course of an editorship.

This leads us to another technique: Fill in the blanks. Take titles from similar pieces in the publication and substitute a word or two. Remember the *Reader's Digest*: "I Am Joe's Stomach" and "Liver" and "Bladder" and on through your biology textbook? The results often aren't ultraoriginal, but the method works. For example, how many articles on regional/national foods have you seen called "A Taste of . . ." or travel pieces titled "_____: An Undiscovered Paradise." They're proof that originality isn't always the name of the title-producing game.

When parodying, rhyming, or using any of the other creative devices, it's a good idea after you have your capsule sentence well thought out to push the whole matter into your subconscious. You'll find that a malleable phrase will pop into your mind at the most unexpected moment—when you're filling the car with gas or walking down the supermarket aisle—and will need only a bit of polishing to work. (Be sure to keep paper and pencil handy.)

Sometimes naming an article happens quite another way. Your article idea may first appear as a full-blown title, flashing through your brain like a streak of summer lightning. When this happens, you'll work from the top down, contriving a lead and capsule sentence that are complementary and in the publication's style.

Paying attention to title length is a must. Most are six words or less. Don't fall into the trap of thinking they *all* are. True, you won't come across many like this one, which appeared in a publication called *Panorama* several years ago: "How I Became a Supporter of and Appalled by Docudrama, and a Fan of the Talented, Frustrated, Confused Men and Women Who Would Like to Make Television Better if Only So They Wouldn't Have to Apologize for What They Do—Write and Produce the Stuff America Loves." But you will see the six-word limit exceeded with regularity, especially in tabloids, whose features often span several columns.

To determine the ideal title length for a particular magazine, copy titles from three to six back issues. A look at the contents pages from three issues of *Midwest Living* will show you how it's done.

DATE	TITLE	TYPE	NUMBER OF WORDS
8/90	Great Lakes Island Odysseys	Label	4
	Pedal-Powered Vacations	Label	3
	Summer Places	Label	2
	Water Garden Wonders	Label	3
	Sweet Corn	Label	2
	How Sweet It Is!	Statement	4
10/90	Hometown Pride Winners	Label	3
	Grand Hideaway Hotels	Label	3
	Autumn Weekend Adventures	Label	3
	St. Paul	Label	2
	Michigan's First Family of Tulips	Label	5
	Settling Into a Frontier Farmhouse	Label	5
	All-Star Dining	Label	3
12/90	Yuletide Treasures	Label	2
	Joys of the Season	Label	4
	Holiday Homes	Label	2
	An Ozark Country Christmas	Label	4
	A Cookie Walk	Label	3
	Holiday Cookbook	Label	2

Of the nineteen titles, eighteen are labels and all but two of them contain from two to four words. Now, let's go through the same procedure with *Nevada*:

DATE	TITLE	TYPE	NUMBER OF WORDS
6/90	Great Nevada Collections	Label	3
	How I Became King of the Slots	Statement	7
	Rodeo Nights	Label	2
	Grand Illusions	Label	2
	Is It a Mirage?	Interrogative	4

Pumping Border to Border	Label	4
In Its Own Image	Label	4
Tom Coleman	Label	2
Poetry and Politics	Label	3
Comstock Yarn Spinners	Label	3
Gardeners of the Purple Sage	Label	5
Nevada Peaks	Label	2
12/90 The Valley Barons	Label	3
The Fine Art of Fine Dining	Label	6
UFOs: The Nelson Chronicles	Label (Two-Parter)	4
Making Mayhem and Merry	Label	4
Rebel's Shot Blocked?	Interrogative	3
The Brothers Grosh	Label	3
House Hunting in a Boom Town	Label	6
1/91 Beyond the Bright Lights	Label	4
The Grand Pappy of Gaming	Label	5
Paving the Way to Paradise	Label	5
A New Stage for the Stars	Label	6
Reeling in Paradise	Label	3
Betting by the Book	Label	4
How to Play the Games	Label	5
Rollin' with the River	Label	4
Welcome to Fantasyland	Statement	3
Wayne Newton: Life On (and Off) the Strip	Label (Two-Parter)	8

Of the twenty-nine titles, twenty-five (86.2 percent) of them have label titles, two of which are two-parters. Of the remaining titles, two are interrogative and two are statements. Word lengths of three to five words predominate (about 69 percent). You'll notice that editor David Moore likes both alliteration and wordplay, as well as straightforward titles.

Though state and regional magazines have an unusually consistent title flavor, staffs of most other publications also have readily discernible title preferences. *Entrepreneurial Woman* is a case in point. A look at the contents page of just one issue tells you a lot about coming up with a perfect title for that editor. "What's Up?" "Do You Hear What I Hear?" "Off and Running," "Beware the Investor," "What Price Ethics?" "Striking a Match," and "The Italian Connection" are the titles in a typical issue. Right away, you'll notice that three of the seven titles are interrogative, while one is an imperative and the remaining three are labels. And don't ignore the fact that all the titles employ a mild amount of wordplay.

A second look reveals that five of the titles have three words in them; one has two, and the other, six. Your best title choice, therefore, would be a three-word interrogative or label, and chances are you would strive for a bit of cleverness.

Title/Lead Compatibility

Deciding what to read first (or what to read later or whether to read the magazine at all) is like impulse buying. We choose whatever strikes our fancy at the moment. I'm sure that if you surveyed magazine readers, you would find few who begin reading at the front and go straight on through the book. Most of us, after glancing at the cover and/or contents page, proceed to turn pages until a title or illustration catches our eye. If it's compelling, we say to ourselves, "That's one I want to read." If it's irresistible—a real grabber—we say, "I've got to read this *right now*."

Therefore, a cardinal rule: The title and lead must be compatible. It's not fair to the reader to promise to tell her about "Money-Making Careers to Start at Home," then not get to the subject until halfway through the piece. Since the title tells what an article is about and the lead introduces and capsulizes that subject, there has to be harmony between the two.

An excellent example of the title/lead tie-in is this one, which appeared in an earlier issue of *Midwest Living* than those surveyed above.

ZOUNDS!
Shakespeare Wows 'em in the Wisconsin Woods
A vacationer guns her way toward the little southwestern Wisconsin town of Spring Green, hoping to make an 8 p.m. performance of the American Players Theatre. She speeds past a landscape of trees and cows, thinking this an unlikely spot for a noted Shakespeare company. The driver doesn't even notice a police car—

lights flashing, siren wailing—closing in on her.

"We're going to see *Hamlet*," she offers lamely, to the bull-necked patrolman. "Not tonight, you ain't," growls the cop, his face jutting close. "Tonight," he says, breaking into a grin, "it's *The Merry Wives of Windsor*."

In this pretty and rustic part of Wisconsin, the Bard of Avon wins enthusiastic audiences of car mechanics, short-order cooks, college profs, and yes, cops. Out-of-towners flock to this outdoor amphitheater, and Lady Macbeth is nearly as well known among locals as Charming Carrie, the county's top milk cow. "It's not that surprising," laughs one member of the company. "These plays weren't written for snobs. They were written for and loved by the common people."

The American Players Theatre is the only professional repertory troupe in the U.S. exclusively performing full-length classical drama . . . .

Although the article's capsule sentence doesn't appear until the fourth paragraph, the reader is led into the Shakespearean tie-in during the second sentence of the anecdotal lead. The next paragraph adds a neat twist that ends the anecdote and cements the title/lead connection. In the third paragraph, the combination of two narrative sentences and an excellent quote amplifies the anecdote. Everything preceding the capsule sentence sets the stage for the subject as set forth in the title.

As you analyze articles, you'll see a strong correlation between title/lead compatibility and well-crafted articles. You will realize that whatever styles and structures editors prefer, they're not buying many articles that lack some sort of title and lead tie-in. Since leads are usually no more than one to two hundred words long, don't fashion the title from material that's buried on the fourth page of the piece (for more on lead lengths, see chapter seven).

Most people's titles aren't lively enough, editors agree. They say that a good title, while providing the reader with some information, has to be interesting enough to keep him reading.

Since there are trends in title fashion, the article designer should update his title research periodically, noting whether his target editors are following trends or continuing their established patterns. No editor will go overboard and abandon the old completely, but the more innovative among them will react positively to your not-quite-traditional efforts.

It sometimes happens that writers fall in love with their titles. They may become so enamored, in fact, that they don't construct solid stories to go with them. Clever titles without good writing backing them have never sold manuscripts. Writers with titlemania may also want to protect their articles' names with copyrights (which isn't possible because titles cannot be copyrighted) and are devastated when editors rechristen their pieces. There's one sure cure for this affliction: the realization that selling your article — whatever it's ultimately called — is certainly better than no sale at all.

The addition of blurbs to many titles poses a question for both beginning and experienced writers. Will it hinder or help their chances if they write blurbs for their pieces? Although this is traditionally the editor's job, there are occasions when you can give her a hand. If I can contrive a *really good* blurb, constructed to fit perfectly into the editorial mold, I type it below my title. When I can't dream up a first-rate blurb (or if the magazine rarely uses them), I don't produce one.

Following the same rule, never include subheads — the segment titles that break up blocks of text — if you haven't seen them in your target magazine. When they're used, subheads are usually written by the editor. If you can provide good ones in her preferred style, the editor won't have to bother, adding more points in your article's favor. The same analytical tools used in dissecting titles can be applied to subheads with the same results — satisfied editors.

And that's the name of the writing game.

Chapter Seven

Great Beginnings and Happy Endings

The beginning is half of the whole.

Plato, *Laws*

The p'int of good writing is knowing when to stop.

L.M. Montgomery, *Anne's House of Dreams*

    A successful freelancer remarked some years ago, "I look at the lead as my first chance. My last chance. My only chance. A mediocre article can make it if you have a great lead but a great article with a dull lead will come boomeranging back for one basic reason. The editor won't bother to read beyond the first dreary paragraph."

    I won't go so far as to say that editors *never* buy articles with dull leads—I've read too many of them. But to my mind, those beginning paragraphs are the writer's best chance for making an editorial conquest. It's like the first lick of an ice cream cone. If that tastes good, you'll be set up to enjoy the whole thing. Of course, the rest of the article can't deteriorate into a mishmash of vagaries or a blob of poorly crafted prose. Chances are, though, if you can write a compelling lead, you'll do a competent job on the rest.

As we've learned, what's good so far as an editor is concerned may not be our own first choice. That goes for leads, too. We might, without analysis, think that one type of lead would be perfect for an article and use it. But if we have learned that the editor in question goes for a different kind of lead 50 percent of the time, a second type, 30 percent, and never *ever* uses the type of lead we have in mind, we won't play our favorites, but his.

It's hard enough, you say, to come up with a lead anytime, let alone when you're restricted by editorial preferences. We've all been brainwashed with the stories about the journalist who put paper into his typewriter, stared at the blank page for two or three days, then, when he finally decided how to begin, wrote the article in half an hour. I have a suspicion that the mystique that has grown up around writing leads, like writer's block, is often used to rationalize our unwillingness to get on with the show.

Lead analysis eliminates that excuse. By knowing what an editor wants, you'll have no reason to stare at that empty page for more than five minutes, nor will you want to.

But first you have to know exactly what a lead is and what it should do. It's the curtain raiser, the attention grabber, usually one to three paragraphs long, that sets the stage for your *capsule* or *nutshell* sentence. This sentence is the statement of the article's theme. It sets forth, in synopsized form, what the writer is going to spend the next five hundred to fifteen hundred words detailing.

The purpose of the lead is to interest, entice and intrigue. It must persuade the reader that the article is more important to her at that moment than shoveling the sidewalk or watching "Monday Night Football." It's your entrée to the reader's time, an entrée you gain by letting her know that what you have to say is important or pleasurable or vital to her well-being.

As you read the leads of the articles in several back copies of your target publication, put an asterisk next to those you find especially effective. Effective or not, note the kind of lead in the margin opposite each one. You'll want these notes for future reference.

I also find it helpful to identify the tone of each lead, whatever its type. I ask myself whether it's low-key or hard-sell; whether the editor likes a lot of razzle-dazzle or prefers a more restrained approach. The tone of a lead should establish the mood or feeling created throughout the entire article. Here are the kinds of leads you are most likely to find.

Summary

One of the most popular leads (and perhaps easiest to write), the summary usually is only a paragraph or two long. It tells, succinctly, what the article is about. Tabloids like the *Star* and *National Enquirer* make extensive use of the short summary lead. Look at an issue of any one of them and you'll find it is filled with articles that begin with one summarizing sentence.

The tabloids aren't the only publications in which this type of lead is popular. You'll find summary leads in almost every magazine on the newsstands today. This one appeared in an article called "Sludge Gains Respect" in *Ford New Holland News*.

> North Carolina's top yielding corn crop in 1988 was produced without the help of nitrogen fertilizer. The winning yield of 259.41 bushels per acre came from land fertilized with only 200 pounds of potash per acre.
> But the unlikely winner of that state's corn growing contest did add one other material to the soil . . . sludge.

And *Paper Collector's Marketplace* printed this one in an article called "Film Goddess of the Thirties," which told about Jean Harlow and paper memorabilia connected with her career.

> Tucked in between Clara Bow and Marilyn Monroe in the "film goddess" hierarchy was an actress named Jean Harlow. Known as "America's Blonde Bombshell" to her many fans, Harlow was perhaps the best known — and certainly one of the most popular — actresses of the 1930s.

Although most summary leads are much shorter, you will

occasionally come across one that's quite long, like this lead from an article called "The Emerging Midwest" in *NASFT Showcase*, a specialty food publication:

> Ironically, one of the richest food regions in the U.S. has something of an identity complex when it comes to its own cooking. The Midwest—historically America's breadbasket—is rethinking its importance in the scheme of regional American cuisines.
>
> "California doesn't borrow food ideas from the Midwest; the Southwest doesn't borrow from the Midwest," says Michael Foley, chef/proprietor of Printer's Row and Foley's in Chicago. "Why should we borrow from other regions?"
>
> Foley, a leading proponent of Midwestern regional food, has recently been joined by an increasingly large number of Midwestern retailers and restauranteurs who are questioning the hegemony of the coastal cuisine idea that everything of culinary importance happens on the coasts. "It's gotten to the point where we're calling this the 'Corn Coast,' " quips Howard Solganik, a Dayton, Ohio-based specialty and retail food consultant.
>
> According to Solganik, Midwestern cuisine is often misjudged because it is not easily identifiable. "Midwestern cuisine can't be isolated as one ethnicity like, say, Creole food," he says. "Midwestern cuisine has more to do with the abundance of good ingredients. We call it 'Corn Bowl Abundance.' "
>
> Due to its strong, often leading, position in corn, wheat, oats, barley, beef, pork and certain vegetables, the Midwest is the headquarters of many of the country's large and small food companies. It is also where many ideas about American food were formed.

In the above example, although the first paragraph sounds a lot like a lead, it really doesn't tell what the article is about—the diversity of Midwestern food products and their marketing.

Interrogative

The interrogative lead asks a question. Its purpose is to make the reader wonder, and in wondering, proceed to read the article.

This example of an extremely short interrogative lead appeared in an astrology magazine called *Jupiter*:

"What determines a lottery winner? Lady Luck in many cases; lucky stars in others."

A series of questions can also be an effective lead, as illustrated by this one from "5 Secrets of (Average-Looking) Women Who Attract Men Like Crazy" in *Woman*.

Sex appeal. What is it? Who's got 'it'? Is sex appeal a glow that surrounds a woman? Are there ways to enhance it?

Since the days of Cleopatra women have pondered these questions. And since the days of that long-ago temptress, *some* women have been sexier than others. What are their secrets?

It's all a matter of what messages a woman sends out.

In this typical series of questions lead, all the queries refer to the focus of the article—sex appeal. The summary sentence following the questions gives the answer, which will be elaborated upon during the remainder of the article.

In this *GQ* article about white buck shoes, the author also leads off with a series of questions:

You know that box of old photographs that your mother has in the hall closet? The one with all the pictures of your great-grandmother's sisters and lots of guys you can't identify in dark suits and hats? Those pictures for which "That's your father's grandfather's brother Emil, the one who fell down the well in 1906" is usually the answer to your questions? Well, I was looking through a batch of such pictures that I inherited when my mother cleaned a closet a while back, and I found this photo of her and my father in Michigan City, Indiana, in the summer of 1938. This was pre-me, and it was apparently before my father had switched to dark-blue suits and black cap-toed shoes as a year-round wardrobe. He's wearing a long-sleeved white shirt, white trousers and white shoes. I was inspired.

If my father, a man to whom dignity came naturally, could wear white shoes, I, by God, could wear white shoes.

Conversational

This kind of lead is effective because of the informality of its approach. It makes the reader feel, "Hey, this guy is talking to *me*." You'll find the conversational lead most often in articles dealing with personal relationships, the outdoors, humorous articles and some how-tos. The following, from an article called "No Mountain High Enough" in *New Woman*, makes good use of the personal, I'll-tell-you-all-about-it approach:

> For 20 years I have approached skiing, my all-time favorite sport, with complete and wholehearted ambivalence. My winter vacations closely parallel Woody Allen's description of life in general: full of pain and suffering, and all over much too quickly. Each year, I spend a large amount of money on a string of petty miseries—numbing cold, graceless tumbles, and hair-raising near-collisions with teenagers in hyperdrive. Still worse: although my skills are good, I remain an abject coward at heart. If the pitch gets steep, I'll suddenly stiffen and cling to the mountain like a treed cat.
>
> And yet, there are those days. . . .
>
> There are those rare days when I suddenly throw away every fear or worry or stress I've ever known and sink into the airy void with utter trust and sheer, dumb delight. For me, skiing has the power to unlock, if only for a moment, a deep reservoir of joy and well-being.
>
> Last March, in an attempt to increase the ratio of good stuff to bad in my skiing experience, I joined a women's ski seminar in Snowmass, Colorado. The concept, according to Debbie Morris, instructor and initiator of the program for the Aspen Ski School, is that the traditional macho approach toward skiing—tough it out, stiff upper lip, attack the mountain—often leaves women cold, in more ways than one.
>
> Debbie has found that women learn best not by stifling their fears but by expressing and working through them in a supportive environment . . . .

It's tough, sometimes, to find the capsule sentence in the conversational lead. At first, you may have to read through most of an article and then go back to figure it out. After you've had a bit of practice, they'll be easier to spot. Even if you can't find the traditional capsule sentence, don't worry. Conversational leads frequently state the article's theme in a group of sentences rather than in a single phrase.

Another conversational lead I like sets the tone for an article called "Paris—Remembrance of Things Past" in *Gourmet*. Actually, it's a conversational lead that begins with a quote.

> "If I had compared my life to a cake, the sojourns in Paris would have represented the chocolate filling. The intervening layers were plain sponge. But my infatuations do not begin at first taste. I nibble, reflect, come back for more, and find myself forever addicted." If I should presume to liken my Paris to A.J. Liebling's, I too could but rejoice in the chocolate butter cream.

The conversational lead is a favorite of (and is often abused by) beginning writers. Their problem seems to stem from the inclusion of too much irrelevant detail, and the results sound amateurish. It is possible, however, by studying good examples, to learn to separate necessary information from that which clutters up the prose.

Narrative

This lead sounds like a storyteller beginning a yarn. It can be crisp or gentle, depending on the subject. Sometimes the narrative lead sounds a bit like the opening paragraphs of an essay. Other times, it provides background material leading up to the subject. One of the most beautifully crafted narrative leads I've ever read appeared years ago in a *National Geographic* article called "The Magic World of Hans Christian Andersen." Though it was written years ago, the work is so timeless that it can serve as a pattern today.

> There's a world, just around the corner of your mind, where reality is an intruder and dreams, the bad along with the good, have a disconcerting way of coming true.
> You can get into this world in many different ways: by tumbling down a rabbit hole or climbing up a beanstalk, by riding a Kansas cyclone over the rainbow—or opening a book of fairy tales by Hans Christian Andersen.
> Of all the travelers who have journeyed to that enchanted realm of once upon a time, none—to my mind—has come back with treasures more glistening than this unlikely Dane, who wrote, "Life itself is the most marvelous fairy tale."

In an entirely different vein, here's a conversational approach to the narrative lead used to begin a profile in *Wigwag*:

> Before I knew Missoula Municipal Court Judge Wallace N. Clark, I knew the women he terrorized. A woman who said he deserves the cancer he now has. A woman who said she wouldn't be sorry to see him die. Women who worked for him as clerks.
>
> I knew Pat Mann, who told me about the time her mother was dying of cancer and Clark refused to give her a leave without pay. I knew Maxine Reese, who would later describe working for Clark this way: "I was physically afraid. I wouldn't have been any more afraid if he had attacked me with a gun, and he did verbally abuse me all the time. . . . It was just a strange feeling. I just shook. I'd come to work and I'd sit at my desk and wonder, When is the hell going to break loose today? What's going to tip it off today?"
>
> But I also knew Michael Moore, the reporter for the *Missoulian* who had taken his Siberian husky with him in 1981 when he appeared before Clark in municipal court after getting a ticket for not having his dog on a leash.
>
> Clark looked at the dog. "That dog doesn't look Irish," he said. "That dog looks Communist."
>
> Moore said that the dog had no Communist leanings that he knew of. "You're Irish," said Clark. "You ought to get an Irish dog." Moore conceded that the dog wasn't Irish, but added that every time he got loose he ran toward Butte (a mostly Irish mining town where the social event of the year is the St. Patrick's Day parade). "Good. He's innocent," said Clark, banging his gavel on the desk.
>
> That's Wally Clark. A man who can inspire the most corrosive hatred and turn on the most compelling charm.

Anecdotal

These ministories are effective ways of introducing a subject, since we all like glimpses into other people's lives. In order to be effective, they must relate directly to the topic by illustrating it, amplifying it, dramatizing it, or by proving a point.

In profiles, the anecdote often serves to illustrate a characteristic of the subject, give the reader a glimpse into the person's early life, or in the case of a celebrity, tell how he or she got the big break. Travel anecdotes frequently relate a travel incident or give insight into the lives of the subject locale's inhabitants. Whatever the subject, the anecdotal lead gives a human-interest quality to the piece, as illustrated in this article called "They Burn Churches, Don't They" in *Woman's Day*.

In the chilly early hours of October 18, 1988, James Russell Calvin crept through a window of Rocky Fork Church. He was 19 then, slender and shy, with reddish-blond hair, a neat mustache and cold eyes. The church stood alone in a clearing, founded 125 years ago by slaves who had followed the Underground Railroad to this spot just outside the town of Alton, in the "free" state of Illinois.

In the autumn night, did the pale young man catch the smell of new wood or fresh paint? Just six months earlier, a person or persons unknown had splashed gasoline on the walls, burning the church to the ground. All that summer, often in 100-degree heat, black and white volunteers had worked to reconstruct the one-room church and its bell tower.

Rocky Fork, as the New Bethel African Methodist Episcopal (A.M.E.) Church is called, was set to reopen for next Sunday's prayers—until Calvin crawled in. "I was going to look around," he confessed to the police and also told an *Alton Telegraph* reporter. He spotted a half-full jar of paint thinner left behind by workmen, and reached for his cigarette lighter.

James Russell Calvin burned Rocky Fork in a violent autumn. In Brooklyn, New York, two teenagers set fire to the Torah scrolls and destroyed the inside of a synagogue. In Portland, Oregon, racist Skinheads—tattooed, jack-booted, violent young people—murdered one black man with baseball bats and injured two others. At Dartmouth College in New Hampshire, threats were sent to black and gay students.

Across the nation, hate crimes—acts of violence committed because of differences in race, religion or sexual preference—are on the increase after years of steady decline.

A shorter anecdotal lead grabbed reader interest in this article about attorney Harriet Rosen in *Lear's*.

In a packed federal courtroom in Lower Manhattan in December of 1986, defense attorney Harriet Rosen interrupts a trial of 22 Sicilian and American Mafia thugs accused of running a billion-dollar heroin ring, known in the tabloids as "The Pizza Connection." The trial is in its 15th month. "I have some overwhelmingly sad news," she says. "My client has been found dead."

Her client, Gaetano (Tommy) Mazzara, missing without a trace for the past five days, had only hours ago turned up dead in a gutter on a Brooklyn street, shot twice in the head and stuffed in a plastic garbage bag.

The capsule sentence appears four paragraphs later in the article, but with a lead like that, you can be sure readers went on to read it.

Case History

The case history is like the anecdotal lead in that it, too, tells a story, or part of one. Although case history leads used to be written most often to introduce articles related to medicine, they have become increasingly popular as openers for articles on everything from office stress to dumping a boyfriend. Here's one from a piece called "What a Baby Does to a Marriage" from *Working Mother*.

Suzanne wakes suddenly from a restless sleep to the wails of her four-month-old son, Jamie. Carefully lifting the covers to get out of bed without waking her husband, she's surprised by the touch of his hand on her arm. "Leave Jamie alone," says Peter firmly. "Let him cry it out, or he'll keep waking us every night." She hesitates, then she asks, "But what if something is wrong?" "There's nothing wrong," snaps Peter. "You're being overprotective."

Talking about the incident the next day with a friend, Suzanne was still upset. Despite Peter's protests, she'd gone to comfort Jamie and fell asleep while nursing him on the cot next to his crib. At breakfast that morning, she and Peter barely spoke. She ran upstairs when Jamie awoke, and the next thing she knew Peter was out the door.

"I don't know what's happening between us," says Suzanne, choking back tears. "This should be one of the happiest times of our lives. Yet I feel my world is starting to fall apart."

After two more paragraphs that summarize what happens when a couple has a baby, the capsule sentence—New parenthood, while usually a joyous event, is likely to be a time of potential crisis—tells readers precisely what the article is about.

The following case history began the lead for an article called "Craving for Change: How to decide if it's time to leave your man, your job or rethink your life" which appeared in *Glamour*.

Karen Haven was twenty-eight when the craving for life change took hold of her. It began slowly, as a nagging restlessness, a mosquito's buzz never quite out of hearing, a vague dissatisfaction with anything and everything.

"I felt anxious and bored at the same time," says Karen. "I couldn't seem to focus on exactly what the problem was. I had a good job, a boyfriend with whom I'd been happily living for three years, interesting women friends. But I kept having this fantasy of being in an entirely different life. I'm not one to make hasty decisions, especially when I'm not miserably unhappy, so I decided to just do nothing and see if my restlessness went away." It didn't, so Karen began to take a good look at her life, starting with her work. She'd been a graphic designer for a large retail store for four years. "I made good money, had good benefits and my boss liked me," she recalls. "I was very comfortable there—maybe *too* comfortable. I'd been ignoring the fact that I was bored to death.

"I realized I didn't want to wake up at forty-five and still be parking my car in the same lot every day, designing the same kind of ads for the same kinds of merchandise. I started to feel that if I stayed there I'd never stretch myself." Within a year, Karen decided to quit her job to work independently.

"The craving for change doesn't occur suddenly," says David Viscott, M.D., director of the Viscott Institute for National Therapy in California. "What seems like a sudden crisis is really an indicator that you haven't been true to yourself for some time. Everyone carries with them a notion of what they should be, but it's often suppressed—until they reach a period of darkness when nothing is motivating them. It's then that you realize you're not fulfilling your dream of yourself."

A common variation of the case history is the series of case histories (usually three), all of which illustrate the article's main thrust.

Statistical

This type of lead is most effective if the statistics are big enough, show contrast, are shocking, or are far different from the average reader's preconception of them. However, during the past few years (perhaps because nothing seems so big or shocks us so much anymore) statistical leads have been used less frequently than they were in the past.

You'll see that statistical leads vary from a short paragraph with only one statistic to this multifigured lead that was used in a *Saturday Evening Post* article called "Circusmania."

> The show must go on, and faced with 340 costumes to press, 130 faces to make up, 28 intricate acts to rehearse, and 240 kids to coordinate, the Peru (Indiana) Amateur Circus needs a lot of help from its friends. So the whole town gets in on the act every year.

Descriptive

This is a favorite with many travel editors. It works especially well if the writer is able to evoke enticing images. Here's one I especially like. It's from a piece called "Chinatown," which appeared in *Motorland*.

> Tiny old women in quilted jackets sit on wooden boxes, quietly gossiping as they fold Chinese-language newspapers. A fishmonger lays row upon glistening row of fresh bass over a bed of crushed ice. Solemn-faced housewives jostle each other as they pick apart produce displays that, moments before, had been artfully arranged geometries of bok choy and fuzzy melons.
>
> Double-parked trucks unload crates of squawking chickens and live crabs that squirm in slow motion. Nearby, a jeweler carefully places jade and gold ornaments on the green felt of his display windows.
>
> When people think of San Francisco's Chinatown, images of pagoda roofs and Grant Avenue souvenir shops come to mind. But that famous avenue — intriguing though it may be — is more of a facade. The real heart of Chinatown is Stockton Street and a web of cross streets and alleys that make up the largest Chinese settlement outside the Orient. And Chinatown's finest hour is

8 a.m., before the tourists arrive, when its 100,000 or so residents begin preparing for a new day.

Descriptions also can lead off articles on processes or inanimate objects, and personality pieces. This descriptive lead appeared in *Spy*. The article was called "Let's Go to the Videotape! (Uh . . . What Videotape?)."

It wasn't a large crowd, but its members were young and bright, and almost all of them tossed their coats over the empty seats as they arrived, lending an air of cozy anticipation to the 63-seat theater at the Museum of Broadcasting. Onstage, two West German producers were introducing their entry in the museum's annual World Television Festival. As the audience peered at the fuzzy image on the screen (a drama about the West German government's surveillance of its citizens), the two producers slipped out for lunch with the museum's television curator to celebrate their heady day in New York.

As soon as the VIPs left, a door to the theater opened and a spotter from the lobby reception desk signaled that the coast was clear. Abruptly, mysteriously, most of the audience members grabbed their coats and began to file out of the auditorium. It may have looked like a Bundestag walkout or an elementary school fire drill, but it was actually a large contingent of the Museum of Broadcasting employees simply going back to work, grateful for yet another house-papering interlude in the otherwise gray job of keeping a deathwatch over the museum.

It turns out that New York's most populist museum, New York's *fun* museum, is run with an altogether appropriate sitcom screwiness.

As in the conversational lead, the capsule sentence in the descriptive lead can be hard to find. In the next example, taken from an article called "Windstar Takes a Different Tack" in *Compass* (the publication of the Marine Office of America Corporation), the capsule sentence is easier to identify.

As the great sailing ship slips away from the shelter of the tropical island, the wind picks up smartly, conveying its direction and intensity to sensors atop the four 200-foot masts. Below, on the bridge of the 440-foot long *Wind Star*, a silent crew member in the form of a Hewlett-Packard 300 computer registers the incoming data and displays them on a large console.

The captain checks the screen, decides that conditions are right and, using a small joystick control like one on a video game, changes the ship's heading slightly to take full advantage of the following wind. Now he punches in a series of commands to the computer, and in less than a minute, six Dacron sails — 21,500 square feet in all — unfurl with celebratory pops as the 12-knot breeze bellies them out.

Gliding smoothly along past the Grenadines, *Wind Star's* heel is barely noticeable, thanks to the computer. It has directed the shifting of tons of water ballast to tanks on the windward side.

The romance of sailing lives on at Windstar Sail Cruises. Founded in 1984, the company is an oddity in today's era of 70,000-ton superships, but judging by an average 80 percent of capacity booked in its first full year of operation, Windstar has found an undeveloped market niche.

Quotation

If good quotes are available, these leads almost write themselves. Usually there is a bit of explanatory prose between the quotation and the capsule sentence, but that sentence can also come directly after the quotation, as it does in the following example from an article in *Architectural Digest*.

When Pauline Kael said of director Robert Altman that "he has the nerve and the genius to try things that nobody else would think of," she had in mind "things" like *M*A*S*H*, *McCabe and Mrs. Miller*, *The Long Goodbye* and *Nashville*.

But now witness, closer to home, his daredevil New York apartment.

In the next example, the capsule sentence is about 150 words away from the quote. The article, called "The Highest Rollers," appeared in *Golf*.

"I live by a credo," says Evel Knievel. "The next best thing to gambling and winning is gambling and losing."

Most $2 Nassau golfers might not see it that way. Some fools might even rate sex, a good meal or even a soft summer night right up there with dropping dough. But the hard-core high rollers live for the action. And for the highest of the high rollers, true action can mean anything from a paltry one-thou-a-hole skins game to a more sobering six-figure Nassau [tournament].

So there's more to daredevil Knievel, we discover, than trying to traverse the Snake River Canyon on a rocket or leaping across a few counties on a motorcycle. Knievel is one of a small fraternity of golfing mavericks who will make a game, hop a plane and head for any course in the country if the price is right. It is not a large group, but that doesn't mean golf gamblers are few and far between. Everyone gambles on golf. Rather, the six-figure regulars are the rare breed.

Here's a third lead illustrating the quotation as curtain raiser. In this case, eight different quotes are used. It's from ''Strength in Numbers,'' an article about cattlemen's marketing clubs, in *Beef Today*.

''It's a cattleman's paradise.''

''Cow-calf pairs are bringing $600 to $850 now. I bought some for $450 to $600 and felt bad.''

''I've never seen cows this fat at this time of year.''

''Short cattle are selling for $91 around here right now.''

''Since there's little risk in the cash calf market right now, I'd just stay open on prices.''

''Estimated break-even on calves kept this fall is a $78.68/cwt. slaughter price next spring if you want to make a $40/head profit.''

''I'd feed heifers—there's a $10-to-$12 steer/heifer replacement spread.''

''I'm looking at selling calves and buying bred heifers or cows to use my pasture instead.''

Those comments and more were heard at the late-summer meeting of the Charlottesville, Va., cattlemen's marketing club. Similar comments can be heard at similar club meetings throughout the U.S., just about any day of the month. Marketing clubs are coming of age.

Another lead you're likely to come across is the *shocker*. It is usually a one-paragraph, summary-type lead that contains information calculated to jar the reader, to make her react with a "Really?" "I can hardly believe that" or "How terrible!" Use of the paradox and of negation are often used in the shocker lead — "It's common knowledge that the more sleep you get, the better you feel. Right? Wrong."

Never use the shocker when your material doesn't warrant it. If you set up your readers to expect thrills, chills and spills, don't give them something that's about as exciting as reading last month's garden club minutes.

Tying your subject to a recent development that has been reported by the media, the *news peg*, works very well with some publications. Other leads you'll find less frequently are the *biographical* and the *definition*. The biographical lead is most common in magazines devoted to history, beginning with the birth of a person or construction of a historic site, then going on to relate important incidents in that life or lifespan. The definition is used to introduce articles whose subjects may not be completely understood without an explanation.

Editors' Choice

There are all sorts of ways you can trigger your typewriter to produce editor-approved leads. I like to start by putting together my capsule sentence. It may not be written exactly as it will appear in the finished draft, but it will be a concise, one-sentence statement of what the article is about. If you can't write such a sentence, it's possible you're going to have trouble writing a satisfactory piece. One writer I know has a sign over his desk, "What in hell are you trying to say?" That question, I've found, is the key to writing. If you aren't *completely clear* about what you want to say, if your ideas are only vaguely formed, the article is going to flop.

After I've settled on the best capsule sentence I can write, I begin asking myself the following questions. In most cases, the lead is written before they're all answered.

1. What leads does this editor like best? Few editors go with the same type of lead for every article, and most of them seem to like two or three kinds particularly well. If you have a choice of two or three types, go with the one that your subject best lends itself to. If none of the editor's favorites seems compatible with your material, write the kind of lead she uses once in awhile.

How do you know which leads dovetail best with your subjects? Check over your material for anecdotes, quotes and statistics. Ask yourself if the subject can be introduced naturally by description or narration or conversationally, and so on down the list of possible choices. The word *naturally* is most important, for in order to be effective, your lead must seem like an integral part of the article—not some words that were tacked on to the front because every piece has to have one. Fortunately, almost all editors print articles with summary leads, at least once in a while, so after you've gone down the list of an editor's pets and all else fails, you'll have one workable option.

Incidentally, if you can't write a summary lead about your subject, you don't have your article well enough in mind to begin writing it.

2. How long are most of the leads? The importance of this answer varies from publication to publication, but it should never be ignored. Woe betide the writer who sends an article with a fifteen-paragraph lead to a magazine that gets into its subjects quickly, say, two paragraphs maximum. *Never* write a lead longer than any you've seen in back issues.

If you have a choice—perhaps the magazine uses leads that vary from one to six paragraphs—opt for a length in balance with the length of your piece. If you can avoid it, don't use a five- or six-paragraph lead on a very short article. You can afford to use more words getting into your subject, however, when the piece is one of the magazine's longest articles.

3. What makes this story important? Since, as we've said, the lead is the grabber, you'll want to do that grabbing as forcefully as you can. What better way to capture the reader's attention than by indicating early on why she must read the story?

4. What is the most interesting facet of the subject? Along with alerting the reader to the subject's importance, you might want to incorporate some fascinating aspect of it in your lead. You probably will touch only briefly on that interesting angle, elaborating upon it later in the text, but the allusion will help snare the reader (and the editor).

Winding Down

Though to many editors they aren't as important as leads, you must give your best effort to constructing endings, too. It's possible to grab an editor with a terrific lead, then lose her with an ending that fizzles. Like the stand-up comic's routine, there has to be consistency in the presentation. If the end of his act goes over like the proverbial lead balloon, the audience won't recall that the first joke was really funny. If your ending has the bounce of a dead tennis ball, your readers (and the editor) won't remember the lead that attracted their attention in the first place.

Most writers find that the midsection of an article is the easiest to write but report they have as much trouble making graceful exits as they do planning grand entrances. Here again, the editor's past choices can come to your rescue.

By studying the kinds of endings your editor prefers, you not only devise patterns to follow, but learn how to write them by a sort of writer's osmosis. Whenever you see a particularly effective one, you'll begin asking yourself why it's so good and what the writer did to make it that way. In the process of studying closings, you'll come across these most popular types.

1. Split Anecdote

In order to end in this fashion, the article must begin with an anecdote. Only part of the story is told in the lead, with the end of it used to wrap up the piece.

2. Summary

This is the closing you'll find most often. It neatly ties the article's contents or conclusion into a synoptic paragraph. Here's one from an article called ''Boom Years Ahead?'' in *Soybean Digest*:

Market forces are set for steady growth in world agriculture. The beginning of this year marks the start of one of the most important 12 months in the history of agriculture. The 1990 Farm Bill and the conclusion of the Uruguay round of the General Agreement on Tariffs and Trade (GATT) will further push world agricultural trade toward a free market economy. More open trading will benefit farmers who are ready to take advantage of opportunities the market offers.

An effective variation of the summary is the full circle, in which the article begins with a summary lead and then reiterates the lead in a summary ending.

3. Urge to Action

Sort of a pep talk, this ending prods the reader to do something about the situation related in the preceding paragraphs and usually tells him how most effectively to take this action.

This closing appeared in *Los Angeles Lawyer* in an article called "Partners in the War on Drugs," which discussed ways in which attorneys can use their special skills to fight illicit drug use:

I hope Los Angeles-area lawyers will join us for these important programs during the Midyear Meeting. They will be an excellent opportunity to learn more about how the drug crisis affects all of us and truly is everyone's problem. Judge Cooper is right. We cannot stand by and say, "Let George do it."

While many urge-to-action endings play upon a sense of duty, others, such as this from "Surrogate Aunts Have *Real* Fun" in *Cosmopolitan*, persuade readers that the action will result in a good time:

So, if you find yourself getting misty-eyed watching diaper commercials, bear this in mind — right now, there's someone out there eager to share your time and affection. And when you light up a child's life, you also light up your own!

4. End of a Sequence

Some topics lend themselves to a series of points or instructions, the last of which is a natural place to end the article. For example, "Killer Patterns," an article in *Cosmo* that dealt with female/male relationships, told about a variety of negative behavior patterns and ended with six suggestions for modification under the heading "How to Stop Sabotaging Yourself." The last point, which follows, brought the piece to a natural close:

> 6. Substitute positive habits for the bad ones you're tossing out. If trying to meet men in singles bars has been causing you heartache, find someplace *else* to snare a date. Or, if you're used to playing clown at the office, save the fun for after hours and try a little *seriousness*.

5. Quotation

Pearls of wisdom pertaining directly to the article's theme can be uttered by an authority on the subject, the person written about, an associate in a personality piece, or a sage of yore. But to keep this type of ending from sounding like a tacked-on whimper, the closing quote must be a strong one.

"Walt LaRue," printed in *Western Horseman*, is a profile about a man who's an artist, actor, singer, stuntman, and former rodeo cowboy. To give readers insights into his subject, the author uses LaRue's quotes liberally, including one as the lead and the one that follows as the ending for the profile.

> Walt is one of those fortunate individuals who have been able to live the life they've wanted to live. "I've enjoyed doing what I've done, a lot of different things. I've been able to paint, and entertain a little, and rodeo, and work in the movies. I could have made a living at any one of them. I've been kinda lucky. I do what I want to do."

In a profile of Norwegian artist Ida Elisabeth in *Viking*, a short quote by the subject brings the article to an appropriate, punchy close:

> Ida Elisabeth seems to enjoy testing the marketing and business theories she picked up while editing textbooks in those subjects when she worked for a publishing company. To Ida Elisabeth, the extra work beyond painting is worthwhile. "I'd rather be a little bit

famous when I'm alive rather than real famous when I'm dead.''

6. For Further Information

The freelancer's favorite, for obvious reasons, this ending is used most often in how-to articles and service pieces that tell about travel. Here's an example:

"For further information about Aruba's beaches and resorts, contact Lou Hammond & Associates, Inc., 39 East Fifty-first Street, New York, New York 10022.''

7. *The Closing Anecdote*

It's superbly effective if you can find a good one, as you can see from this piece about leads called "In the Beginning . . . " in the *Atlantic*. The article, after discussing the first words of a dozen or so famous writers, acknowledged H.L. Mencken to be one of the greatest lead writers of all time. It closed this way:

. . . Mencken's first sentences are in competition with the rest of his pieces, and to my mind, the first sentences win every time.

The effort to make good on the promise of the first sentence, which was too much for Mencken, must stanch innumerable pieces of writing before they have fairly begun. That is because it's possible to write a first sentence that just has to be the last sentence, the last word, on that subject, since it says everything about it in a way that is instantly perceivable as complete. I say it's possible because I have heard of such a case. A distinguished British newspaper proprietor had died, and his paper was under the competitive necessity of making as much of his death as a very liberal hyperbole would allow. So the editor summoned the paper's best writer and drummed into him the herculean expectations the paper had for the obituary he was to write. The writer, who was known to possess a lubricable genius, was taken to a hotel room, furnished with a typewriter and paper, and locked in for the night. Early the next morning the editor opened the door to find the writer slumped over his typewriter, asleep, an empty whiskey bottle at his feet. The room was littered with crumpled sheets of paper and on the sheet in the typewriter were these words: "Not since the death of Jesus Christ . . . ."

Whether you're writing for *Pizza Today* or UPB, *The Voice of the United Polka Boosters*, whatever kind of ending your analysis indicates is right for a piece, it must be a logical conclusion and an integral part of the whole. Carol Amen, whose articles have appeared in dozens of publications including *Ford Times*, *Modern Maturity* and *California Living*, says, "One thing I try to do, and remind my students of this also, is to go back to the beginning and see what I have delivered, and to tie up the loose ends. If there was a person with a problem in the opening, I may put that same person, and some workable solution or way to live with the problem, in the final paragraph. The aim is to provide resolution."

Freelancer Helen Bottel's goal, too, is to tie things up in her last paragraph, relating back to the beginning, using a pithy comment or quote that may add a dimension and, she hopes, make people think. She illustrates her point with excerpts from an article called "Helping Your Teens to Handle Today's Sex Freedom," which first appeared in *Family Circle* and was later condensed in *Reader's Digest*. The lead began:

> Too many adults view the New Morality as the New Immorality and fear has driven them into a square box where they either cower or fight blind. . . . What CAN we, as parents, say to our progeny about sex, especially premarital sex?

And the ending reads:

> Put your arguments as questions . . . Don't force discussions . . . Just be there — and let your child know that no subject will ever be off limits. His ideas may clash with the old way, but if you have raised him with honesty and affection, stop worrying. He may not choose exactly the route you hope, but he will be true to your standards for his time and place.

Through my writing years, I have collected leads and closings that, like Bottel's, are especially effective. You may want to also. To keep them in simple-to-use form, just divide a three-ring binder into sections, with tabs indicating the different types of beginnings and endings. When you find good examples, clip them out, write the publication's name and date, and then tape them to blank pages. Filed according to type, these "patterns" will guide you when the time comes to write your own. In all probability, you'll actually enjoy writing the first and last paragraphs of your pieces. For by using analysis, those beginnings and endings will lead to the beginning of gratifying editorial relationships.

Chapter Eight

Wrapping It Up with Analysis

Little do such men know the toil, the pains,
The daily, nightly racking of the brains,
To range the thoughts, the matter to digest,
To cull fit phrases, and reject the rest.

Charles Churchill, *Gotham*

*T*he only argument I've heard against analysis is that it "kills spontaneity." I can counter that one. Spontaneity, as far as my experience (and that of other writers I've talked with) is concerned, hasn't sold many articles. In fact, doing what comes naturally is what keeps many writers—especially nonfiction writers—from selling.

Instead of producing spontaneous creations, you want to put your material into analytically on-target, rejection-proof form. You have your subject and markets well researched; perhaps there's even a go-ahead on speculation. Your title and lead

109

are firmly in mind, and you have culled every possible clue to the editor's preferences from previously published articles. What remains to be done is to get the article together: written from beginning to end, prepared for submission, and shipped off to the magazine.

Just as each editor has favorite styles and title, lead and ending types, so does he or she have preferred structural patterns. To say that all any writer needs to know about article construction is that there must be a beginning, middle and end is a statement of omission. And to believe that the writer, as long as he constructs the beginning, middle and end, can do anything his fancy chooses within that structure, is a form of rejection wish.

Since every article poses different problems, your organizational techniques will of necessity vary from piece to piece. One thing is certain, though: To work efficiently and achieve success, an article's construction cannot be a hit-or-miss proposition. The whole job goes more quickly and smoothly, I've found, when my material is in good order.

Getting It Together

The only hard-and-fast rule in organizing your material is that it should be assembled in one place. I like to take my notes in spiral notebooks, consolidating all the research for a piece in one book. Other writers favor steno pads, file cards, ruled legal tablets, or bits and pieces of scratch paper. But unless we can lay our hands on all those notes when we're ready to write, we'll have chaos whatever method of note-taking we use.

As I read over my notes, I evaluate the importance of each bit of information. If it's vital to the piece, I circle a number 1 in the margin opposite. I identify all my material with either a 1, 2, 3 or 4, depending on the necessity of its being included. When, upon review, I find a particularly strong quote or an impressive statistic, I mark it with an asterisk. As I'm reading over my notes, I coordinate the various pieces of information by writing key words in the margin. These indicate which point the material pertains to. As I'm flipping the pages, I often think it would be easier to use cards, but when I've finished the piece, I'm thankful I can file that notebook away (contents clearly marked on the front cover) and not have to worry about losing any odd pieces of paper that might come in handy when I write another piece on a closely related subject.

Many of the tidbits we gather in the course of research are so fascinating that we hate to leave them out. But unless these little gems are germane, unless they contribute to the basic theme of the article (or unless the editor is one who likes a touch of the not-exactly-extraneous-but-almost), you'll find that they should be eliminated. Deciding what research material to include isn't difficult when you study published articles to see what information is important. If an editor has shown a preference for government statistics, use them. If he goes for statements from corporate executives, you'll want to include some, too. Perhaps he likes lots of facts in a sidebar.

Sidebars, in fact, are becoming a fact of editorial life. Used increasingly of late, they're handy devices for relaying information that would otherwise break up the flow of an article. For example, in a recent article that I wrote on manners, which featured advice from gourmet restaurant maître d's and wine stewards, I included one sidebar called "A Gourmet Room Cast of Characters" and another called "To Use or Not to Use Your Fingers and Other Sticky Questions."

At some time during the research-evaluating process, I may put together a rough outline, which includes a list of ingredients. Both the outline and ingredient list follow as closely as possible the format my boss of the moment favors. It might look something like this:

I. Lead (two paragraphs — interrogative, first choice; summary, second; quotation, third — likes quotes from government officials)

II. Two paragraphs of general information on the subject (Substantiate with statistics from the Department of Labor)

III. Subpoint #1 (Illustrate with anecdote)
   A. Paragraph of explanatory text about subpoint
   B. Substantiating paragraph with quotes from two authorities
   C. Contradictory information from business sector with quote from corporate head

IV. Subpoint #2
   A. More government agency statistics with rebuttal from business sector containing statistics they have compiled plus some hard-hitting comments from a second business executive
   B. Analysis of these conflicting stats by an economist

V. Closing (one paragraph summary, first choice; quotation, second; for further information also possible)

This outline illustrates only a few of the structural details you should be on the alert for when analyzing an article's structure. Determine at what point the basic questions—who, where, when, what, why and how—are answered. If the writer is established as an authority, take notice of the part of the article in which this is done, and how. Look at the pacing. While there are editors who delight in copy packed with information, they have colleagues who want to give the reader a rest now and then.

Ask yourself how the theme is developed (remember, that's the succinct capsule sentence that ended the lead). Perhaps it's in the *New York Times* style (expository statement beginning each paragraph, followed by supporting information). Or it may, in the case of historical articles or accounts of contemporary history, be developed in a chronological sequence. Another technique you'll find is the dramatic-incident opening, followed by an explanation of events leading up to the episode, then an elaboration on the dramatized incident.

Check for facts, explanations and opinions, noting where they are located in the text. If the article involves controversy, in what part of the article is it introduced? Where are negative and positive concepts set forth? If the writer wishes her reader to empathize with her subject (or feel antipathy), when does she insert information calculated to achieve this aim? How many points should be covered and what proportion of the article should be devoted to each of them?

If you've done your research well, you will have far more information than you can possibly use. Beginning writers try to include everything. But it's like struggling to pack clothes for a six-week trip into an overnight case. Everything won't fit where you'd like it to. The successful writer, like the experienced designer, learns to fashion his material so there's enough to cover the subject properly but no more than the customer (alias editor) demands.

Once you've done most of your research and drafted your outline, it's possible to begin writing the third paragraph, the eighth—anyplace in the article that seems easiest. There's no rule saying a writer must begin a piece by writing the lead. Some writers find it simpler to start in the middle or final paragraphs. I have written articles that I began with the ending, chipped away at the body, and finished with a lead; other times I've worked the "proper" way. There are occasions when one good sentence pops into your head. When that happens, start with that sentence and flesh out your article in whichever direction is easiest for you.

I type bits and snatches of what I'll need on my word processor, then fill them out until they become paragraphs without worrying at all about the way what I'm writing will fit in, only knowing that it is essential to the piece. I leave about four spaces between each paragraph.

Though more often than not I've typed the material sequentially, there are paragraphs that will fit better in places other than where I had originally intended for them to go. So when I have typed perhaps one half or three fourths of the material I know will be necessary, I start moving the paragraphs around into a progression that makes sense.

If you don't have a word processor, you can use the same method by taking your typed papers and cutting between paragraphs. Insert these paragraphs into the appropriate spots, attaching them with transparent tape (staples and rubber cement work, too), and add a few inches of plain paper when you decide that additional material should follow. This cut-and-paste technique saves hours of retyping and allows you to do all but the final draft without having to redo complete pages.

Sometimes you'll find that you have to perform major surgery, cutting and taping several times until you get a piece flowing just the way you want it to (when I'm having real trouble with a piece, I still do actual cutting and pasting despite having a word processor). The virtue of the cut-and-paste method is that you can work your material in jigsaw-puzzle fashion, interchanging the parts until they fit.

Keep It Rolling

No matter what sort of structure he uses, the successful writer must have a feel for copy flow. His articles have to be written in such a way that they pull the reader smoothly along. To accomplish this seemingly effortless journey from lead to final paragraph, the writer has to have a way with *transitions*. They're the phrases that take the reader from one paragraph or subject to another — the continuity words.

Not all editors share the same favorites for smoothing out their readers' paths, so again, you'll want to find out which transitions your editor likes best. Some of the most common ones you will find in the course of your analysis are:

1. Words or Phrases that Move the Action Forward

For example *second, furthermore, besides, another*; or that connote the passing of time — *on his next visit, the following day*.

2. Repetition of Last Point

Paragraph ends with the sentence, "Thousands of people today are jeopardizing their careers because they are unable to make decisions." First sentence of the next paragraph begins, "Not only are thousands of people suffering from the inability to make decisions . . . ," and goes on to make the next point.

3. Repetition of Key Words

A paragraph ends with the word *anxiety*. The first sentence of the next paragraph: "That same look of anxiety was on her face the next time I saw Nancy."

4. Summation of Last Point and Bridge to the Next

"While there are times when you will need to assume a passive role, it's a good idea to express a conflicting opinion if your convictions are strong" could be the sentence following a paragraph in which assumption of a passive role is discussed.

5. Question Referring to the Last Paragraph

"Why is it that . . . ," "How do you . . . ?"

6. Option to Reader

Whether, If you choose to.

7. Chronological

These transitions seem to fall into place naturally. Paragraphs begin with words and phrases like *Next year, After he had moved west, Following months of backbreaking toil.*

8. Numbered steps

Many how-to articles need few transitions if the steps in the procedure are numbered. When transitions are necessary they are usually of the "in order to," "after you have," and "before you" variety.

9. Location or Method of Transportation

Most commonly used in travel pieces, these include such phrases as "Around the corner from," "A few blocks away you'll find," "On the other side of the city," "You can go by bus to."

10. Naturals

In some articles, material can be arranged so well sequentially that actual words of transition aren't necessary. These pieces are like old buildings whose stones fit so precisely that they were constructed without mortar. Skillful crafting is required to make one paragraph flow neatly to another, but the effect gives a continuity to the reading that results in superior articles.

However skillfully they're constructed, some articles require many more transitions than others. There are editors—particularly those with newspaper backgrounds—who prefer short paragraphs in order to break up columns of type with white space or to facilitate reading. Others don't bat an eyelash at paragraphs of 150 to 200 words. No matter how much paragraphing you have to do to conform to the editor's wishes, make each transition as smooth as you possibly can.

If you have trouble coming up with a perfect transition, look at that problem as a warning flag. An analysis may reveal that the material isn't arranged as logically as it might be. Or perhaps the problem stems from a gap—a whole paragraph or two of information that's needed to expedite the flow and give continuity to the piece.

Dots and Dashes

There are editors and writers who look at punctuation as an adjunct of style. It is. But it's also an element of structure, since punctuation not only contributes to the way words read, but to the mechanics of the article as well.

Look at the dash, for instance. It's a stylistic device, to be sure. In some publications, however, you'll never find one of them. Some editors prefer semicolons instead. Or they might want writers to confine their pause symbols to commas. You can easily discover punctuation preferences by reading what has been published.

And then there's the much-debated exclamation point. Editors seem to either adore or abhor it. I've come across pieces where virtually every other paragraph ends with an exclamatory mark. I've gone through a year's back copies of other magazines where there's not one to be found. As a general rule, editors feel that if the sentence is constructed correctly, there's no need for the mark symbolizing enthusiasm at its end; the enthusiasm is in the placement of the words.

You can be certain that each editor has clearly defined rules as to how material should be punctuated. Since you'll rarely find this information in a magazine's guidelines for writers, the only way you will uncover it is by reading the publication.

Not only do editors have punctuation preferences, few of them suffer typos and grammatical errors gladly. Some of them are downright fanatical about mistakes. Although the following excerpt from a *Wall Street Journal* article refers to staffers' errors, you can be pretty sure that the subject editor—and lots of editors like him—won't expect errors from writers they publish either.

If I worked for Scott DiGarmo, this sent*nce* alone, would cost me at least $550.

That's $25 for garbling "sentence," $25 for the extraneous comma after "alone" and $500 for fumbling the guy's name.

Mr. DeGarmo—that's correct now; I checked it twice—is pulling his purse strings tight on lazy writing. At *Success*, the magazine he runs, Mr. DeGarmo recently began fining senior editors for approving articles containing typographical and grammatical mistakes. He charges $25 for misused commas and hyphens after "ly" words (as in "hastily-conceived"). Most typos also cost $25, but the price for misspelling the name of the main person in a story is $500—minimum.

The Finished Product

When your punctuation is just what the editor ordered and all your material is in perfect sequence, you're ready for the final draft. Though your first-through-your-umpteenth draft-in-one may look like a survivor of battle, that finished manuscript must not. I am convinced that the marginal manuscript that sells does so because it is legibly typed in the prescribed fashion.

Why, you ask, should you spend all that time painstakingly typing a manuscript the editor is going to mark up anyway? First of all, contrary to rumors, editors don't buy manuscripts scribbled on the backs of cereal boxes. Even if the editor has agreed in advance to buy the article, until that check is in your account, you're still a salesperson and you'd better have your shoes shined.

Second, a neat manuscript projects a successful, professional image. A sloppy, unorthodox presentation tells the editor you're an amateur at best, incompetent or really weird at worst. It may seem unbelievable, but I have seen submitted "manuscripts" handwritten on both sides of several sheets of 4×7-inch notepaper (complete with garlands of flowers at the top) or typewritten in red on fluorescent green pages.

Finally, you're looking for repeat business. It's much easier to edit an article without typos, with proper margins and spacing between lines of type. If an editor finds your material easy to work with, it's an incentive to buy more in the future.

Your paper should be standard-sized computer or typing

paper (that's 8½ × 11-inch, with 20-pound bond recommended). If you type your manuscript, your typewriter ribbon must be new so that the print is easy to see. Whether you use a word processor or typewriter, in the upper left-hand corner of the first page, single-space your name, address, and *telephone number with area code*. The phone number is terribly important, as we who have analyzed the publishing world know. Many editors detest dictating letters (or writing them themselves), and they often don't have time to wait for correspondence to make the round trip. If those editors have a telephone number so they can pick up the phone and finish their business in minutes, your chances of a sale skyrocket. Like most people, lots of editors I know act on impulse. And what's the greatest impulse tool around? The telephone.

Another professional touch is to include your social security number with the above information. It intimates that your work is salable and will save the editor time when he does the paperwork to expedite your payment.

In the upper right-hand corner, type *about* or *approximately*, followed by your word count (rounded off to the nearest ten). One third of the way down the page, center your title in capital letters. Whether you underline it or not isn't important. Just as double- and triple-spacing allow room for editing, that third of a page of white space at the beginning of the article leaves room for the editor to write type specifications for the printer (and a new title if yours isn't the one she wants). If a magazine often uses blurbs between titles and articles, you may want to put one there—provided it is a strong one and in the magazine's style. Two spaces under the title or blurb is your by-line as you wish it to appear. The article itself should start three spaces below the by-line.

The general rule in typing manuscripts is to double-space. You'll want, however, to check the writer's guidelines for that publication to be sure. Some magazines specify triple-spacing or three spaces between paragraphs. Others ask for a certain number of characters on each line. Whatever is asked for, supply it.

Caroline Hadley, former editor of *Nevada Magazine* and now a full-time freelancer, feels that even if an editor doesn't ask for a specific number of characters per line, setting up your manuscript that way "is super for an editor if you do it right." Ninety-nine percent of the national and special interest magazines published today use a three-column format, she says, and while the type size may vary—publications for children and the elderly are printed in larger type—it's usually constant, or predominantly so, in a particular publication. Just count the number of letters and spaces in a line.

Although left-hand margins of one inch and right-hand and bottom margins of 1½ inches are suggested in most instructions for manuscript preparation, editors I've talked to say that they prefer more white space. So when you're typing, set up your margins so that they're at least half an inch wider than the rules prescribe. What you want to do is produce pages of copy that are as easy as possible for the editor to read, edit, and mark for typesetters.

On succeeding pages of your manuscript, type your name in the upper left-hand corner. On the next line under that, type an identifying word or slug, say, *Norway* in a piece called "Norway—Scandinavian Delight," *Backpacking* or *Bicycle* for an article titled "Bicycle Backpacking." The reason for the two-choice slug is that if the article were submitted to a backpacking publication, *Backpacking* wouldn't be definitive enough to set your piece apart from hundreds of others the magazine publishes, whereas *Bicycle* would. On the other hand, if the piece were submitted to a bicycling magazine, the *Bicycle* slug wouldn't serve to identify a sheet of paper as part of your piece if dozens of manuscripts accidentally were mixed together. Following the slug, type a dash and the page number.

Move the carriage or cursor down at least four more spaces before you begin the manuscript typing on these pages. Two or three spaces below the final line of your article, use some symbol to indicate that there is no more. I use a series of spaced asterisks (* * *). You can write "The End" if you wish, or type "- 30 -" (newspaper shorthand for the end of copy).

Package your color transparencies in the plastic-pocketed sheets available at photo supply stores. Protect black-and-white glossies with sheets of cardboard. And on the manila envelope containing photos, write in impossible-to-miss large, legible printing, PHOTOS—PLEASE DO NOT BEND.

To further project your image as an experienced writer, include a cover letter with the manuscript and/or photos. You can use typewriter paper, but your letters will look more professional if they're typed on businesslike letterhead. The cover letter can be a short paragraph and shouldn't be longer than three, unless some unusual circumstance warrants it. Refer to the contents and why you're sending them: "In response to your request of May 23 that I submit 'Bizarre Bazaar Bargaining' to you for consideration, I have enclosed the manuscript along with a selection of color transparencies. I hope it's what you have in mind." Be *sure* to spell the editor's name correctly. Many editors state flatly that if an article is sent on speculation or is unsolicited, they will reject it if their name isn't spelled right. This isn't as egotistical or arbitrary as it may seem. After all, if a writer hasn't spelled the editor's name correctly, there is no reason to assume that the other information—names, dates, statistics, directions—is accurate either.

When a manuscript bounces back with a rejection slip (or is held eleven months by an editor before she decides she doesn't want it) send the query out to another magazine that very day. *Don't send the manuscript*. There are certain changes, minor or major revisions, that need to be made before it will be just right for your second, third, or fourth market choice. Whenever you send a manuscript following a go-ahead on speculation, be sure to include a self-addressed envelope with adequate postage attached.

When your article is forced to make the rounds, redo every page that looks less than virginal. There's no point in letting an editor know he's getting merchandise another editor turned down.

Account Book Analysis

Picture yourself down the writing road a piece. Analysis is paying off. You're coming up with more ideas and selling more articles than ever before. As a producing writer with articles in all stages of completion—from queries awaiting editors' responses to finished manuscripts in the mail—you've encountered a new problem: Keeping track of your work.

Since recordkeeping is vital to the professional writer's business, you'll want to analyze not only magazine articles, but your bookkeeping procedures as well. Time is money when you're self-employed, so you'll want a system that's the most efficient for you. It may not be the one the freelancer across town uses; it might be one nobody else in the world is comfortable with. But if it suits your working habits and does the job, that's enough.

Many writers use ledgers, entering submission dates of articles and results, expenses, and income in the columns. One writer I know uses a daybook, making entries daily and attaching receipts to the appropriate pages. Those systems simply do not work for me. My system may not work for you, but some variation of it might.

I prefer a filing system that allows me to keep all my records in two metal recipe card files and a larger accordion-type file. One of the recipe card files has dividers that read *Queries, Work in Progress, Submitted Manuscripts* and *Ideas*.

Most of my articles start out with idea cards. Whenever I have an idea for a piece, I jot the idea, the article's working title, and any snippets of information I may have on a 3 × 5-inch card. It's impossible to remember all the wisps of inspiration floating through your brain, so it is imperative that you write them down before they're lost forever. When I have collected enough material on a particular topic in a file folder with the corresponding working title on it, I write the query. The name of the article appears at the top of a 3 × 5-inch card that I place in the *Query* file. Under the title, I write the publication submitted to and the date, leaving room for the date I will receive word of any action (acceptance, assignment on spec, rejection) on the piece. If the query is rejected, I resubmit it to another editor, making appropriate entries on the next line of the card.

As the article idea progresses from query to acceptance on assignment or speculation, the due date is added and its card is moved to the *Work in Progress* section. When the piece is in the mail, the card moves to *Submitted Manuscripts*, with the date of submission duly recorded. When I am notified by the editor that the article is acceptable, with no rewriting or additional information required, I jot that date midway down the card, along with the amount I'm supposed to be paid. When I receive the check,

I mark "paid" next to that figure, along with the date.

The second recipe card file is my favorite. In fact, when I need an ego boost, I take it out and look at the cards it contains. This is my success file. Separating it into sections are alphabet divider cards behind which I file my sales. Sometimes I get a bit premature and move a card into this file when I've been notified of acceptance, but before I've been paid. This, sadly, is a mistake. Magazines stop publication or change hands overnight, at which times it is questionable you'll *ever* get paid. A new editor may come on the scene, and unless you have a written agreement, you won't have made the sale if he or she doesn't like the piece.

My larger, accordion-type file measures about 8 × 10 inches and has twelve compartments. Originally, the tabs between compartments said things like Dental Bills, Utility Receipts, and Car Maintenance Records. I covered them over with gummed package tape and made my own: *Postage, Office Supplies, Research Materials, Travel, Gasoline, Photography, Telephone, Admissions, Lodging, Dining, Photocopies* and *Income Receipts*. Whenever the spirit moves me (usually when the pile is so huge that my desk becomes inoperative), I file all my receipts in the appropriate slots. It makes the job of recapitulating income and expenses an easy one at income tax time (I put a 3 × 5-inch card listing publication, date, and amount in the income compartment for any article sale whose check doesn't have a receipt portion).

What expenses you can charge off are a matter for you and your accountant to decide, and your labels might differ from mine. Whatever they are, be scrupulous about keeping receipts for every expense that might be deductible. At year's end, you can put the file's contents into a manila envelope, label it with the year, and start filling your file again. (A book you may find helpful in dealing with the business side of your writing is *The Complete Handbook for Freelance Writers* by Kay Cassill. Regarding taxes, consult *The Writer's Legal Guide* by Tad Crawford or *Law and the Writer* by Kirk Polking and Leonard S. Meranus.)

Even if you aren't in need of an ego trip, it's a good idea to analyze your productivity every now and then. Like many other writers, I keep track of how many hours it takes to do each piece. I include time spent interviewing, researching, traveling, writing and for concentrated thinking. I don't count the minutes my brain is wrestling with the article while I'm stirring spaghetti sauce or knitting a sweater, since the piece isn't my primary project during that time.

What constitutes profitable allocation of time will change as your success quotient and reputation grow. You will find that some articles are virtual money-losers because they take so much more time that you otherwise could spend putting together articles for more lucrative markets.

Other pieces, even though they may bring in only fifty or seventy-five dollars are winners because you may be able to research and write them so quickly. I frequently do restaurant reviews for seventy-five dollars each that involve eating time plus no more than an hour to write. Unless I eat very slowly, my payment per hour averages out to about twenty-five dollars, which I consider a totally acceptable wage.

If you're working on a big writing project, these short pieces often provide a welcome change of pace plus the reassuring sight of checks coming in every once in a while.

Your life circumstances will also dictate what is profitable to produce. If you have the time for extensive research and interviewing, big pieces may bring you more money and gratification. Writers who hold full- or part-time jobs often find that doing several short pieces in lieu of a few longer ones works in best with their schedules. But long article or short, you'll utilize your time most efficiently if you let analysis help you with the writing.

Chapter Nine

Spotting the Best Sellers

> *A man is quite dishonorable to sell himself*
> *For anything other than quite a lot of pelf.*
>
> Ogden Nash, *Tide*, November 8, 1946

What kind of magazine articles do you like best? I'll bet I can guess. You like pieces that let you peek into other people's lives. Articles that tell you how to make something that doesn't look homemade or how to solve a personal problem that's been bugging you for a long time. Articles transmitting information so painlessly that they're more like entertainment.

They are the articles I prefer, too, along with most people who read magazines. They're today's best sellers—the kinds of articles editors want to buy because they are the ones that sell magazines.

Personality Traits

The most popular personality pieces, according to the updated Emerson system, can be divided into four types: *profiles* (individual or group), *question-and-answer interviews, individuals overcoming adversity/changing lifestyles/contributing to society*, and *roundups*.

Profile is distinguished from other personality pieces by its depth. Comments from business associates, family, friends, employees, fellow workers and other people acquainted in varying degrees with the subject, who relate to him on various levels, give rounded, total personality coverage. The profile is also closer to biography than any of the other personality pieces.

The *question-and-answer* piece usually involves ten to twenty questions posed by the writer and answered by the article's subject. The article might feature questions asked of Ralph Lauren on the direction of fashion in the twenty-first century. Or it might consist of questions asked of four or five "authorities" in a particular field, be they chefs, nuclear scientists or mothers.

It's said that Gertrude Stein's last words to Alice B. Toklas's query, "What is the answer?" was "In that case, what is the question?" As a personality piece writer, you had better be sure that you ask the right questions, as the success of this kind of article hinges on them. It's not so hard as you might think if you take time to read past articles and formulate the same kinds of questions their authors have asked.

The *individuals (or groups) overcoming adversity/changing lifestyles/contributing to society* pieces have become editorial staples over the past decade. They can chronicle everything, from a divorced father's fight to create a normal family life for his children to an urban family's move to rural America to an octogenarian's crusade against drug abuse.

The *roundup* is a series of people stories with a common theme. Often, the elements of the other personality piece types can be used in the roundup format—for example, a piece telling about five couples who completely changed lifestyles upon retirement; an article showing how various people around the country contributed to the quality of their communities' life.

People piece writers don't have to have access to celebrities, although lots of ink is devoted to them. Look instead for people who have interesting jobs, unusual hobbies, or inspiring philosophies; for people who have won lotteries or lost fortunes and have managed to go on living exemplary lives. If you think a person is fascinating, chances are editors and readers will, too.

Hints on How-tos

Simply stated, there are two basic kinds of how-to articles: *project* and *problem-solving*. How-to writing, especially in presenting a project, is straightforward and doesn't demand great literary skill. It does, however, require an ability to explain processes clearly. It is easier for many writers to describe a lovely spring day than the steps involved in tying one's shoe. But all writers can learn to explain processes easily if they will study the how-tos previously published in their targeted magazines and adapt the terminology to the procedures they're writing about.

Though the form may vary slightly, point-by-point *project* how-tos almost always share several elements. The project is described in the first paragraph, or at least an allusion is made to it, followed by more explanation in succeeding paragraphs. After that, you'll find at least one sentence encouraging the reader to tackle the project and spelling out the advantages of doing it, and another reassuring him that it is not hard to do. The instructions come next.

The procedures for most project how-tos are broken down into consecutively numbered steps. Other techniques include using bullets instead of numbers and beginning each step with boldface type. Each step is explained as it is introduced. How fully each step is explained depends on the readers' skill and experience levels.

Notice that there's never any backtracking. Steps are presented in the order in which they are performed. You'll lose a lot of readers—in more ways than one—if you write a piece that says, "Oh, I forgot to tell you back there when you were hooking up wire B to terminal A that you had better turn off the electricity unless you want a thousand-volt jolt."

Problem-solving how-tos usually fall into five types:

1. How a certain person solved his or her problem. By telling one person's story, the writer gives readers information they can use to solve a similar problem.

2. The case history. This technique is used most often in dealing with psychological or health problems. The names of the people in the case histories are usually fictitious, but their stories should be true. (Some writers admit that not all their case histories actually happened, that they are composites created from information obtained through experts.) Several case histories with accompanying comments are also popular.

3. Point-by-point advice. A few paragraphs of prose, followed by points that are numbered or bulleted, make this format easy to duplicate. Even if numbers or bullets aren't used, you'll find that each point is amplified before going on to the next. Though it's not an infallible rule, most editors don't care for more than a dozen points and rarely use articles with less than five.

4. Advice from an expert or celebrity (either by the expert or celebrity, coauthored, or as told to). When Bessie Brown who lives down the block goes on a diet, it's not news—unless Bessie weighed 534 pounds and lost half of it in six months. But when Oprah takes off fifty pounds (or in the tabloid's words, "goes on a secret diet"), the story can sell to any of a couple hundred publications. One would think that diet articles (or those dealing with children from previous marriages or dozens of other beaten-to-death subjects) would sell about as well as bicycles in the Himalayas. But if you have access to a celebrity or to an expert who can tell readers how to do something that's important to them, it's a good bet you'll not only sell the article, you'll make better than average money doing it.

5. Anecdotes in series. These are little stories told in sequence, each illustrating a point or group of points pertaining to a single subject. The anecdotal approach differs from the case study in that it is less clinical. In fact, anecdotes can do a lot to lighten an otherwise somber subject. The writer cements these anecdotes together with reinforcing quotes from experts, statistics, and expository material that moves the piece from one story to the next.

Personal anecdotes can involve more than your own health, looks and social life. They extend to your finances, putting up with a difficult boss, getting along with your in-laws.

Information, Please

It would be safe to say that all articles worth reading are informational in that they contain knowledge. The profile relays information about the featured person. How-tos supply information on making tangible products, solving problems or executing tasks.

Nonetheless, we use the category informational article for pieces whose sole purpose is to tell about something, be it tide-pool life or a new kind of staple gun, Tivoli Gardens or starfruit.

Informational articles have a bigger market than any other. In fact, it would be difficult to find a magazine that doesn't print these articles in every issue. City magazines and regional publications are full of them, for they are information advance men. Their job is to tell readers about the city, state, or region—where to buy the biggest pumpkins, the best secondhand clothes, the most delicious hamburger; where to see magnificent rock formations, catch enormous fish, or get away from it all.

Travel magazines' subscriptions depend on telling readers about places and travel pleasures around the globe. Business magazines without informational articles would result in thousands of frustrated subscribers and plummeting sales. Women's magazines, natural science and outdoors publications, sports, theater and children's magazines, Sunday supplements and newspaper features depend heavily on pieces that give their readers the facts. Without informational articles, the raison d'être of technical and trade journals would vanish. Collectors, whether they specialize in coins, antiques, bottles or barbed wire; people who want to improve their health; car lovers, cat fanciers—all want to know more about their special interests.

An informational article's primary function, as we have mentioned, is to transmit knowledge. This is not to say that the informational piece can't be entertaining or humorous. But whatever its style, the article must, if it's a good one, leave the reader feeling that he or she has learned something.

There are five basic types of informational articles: *expository, investigative, evaluation/review, exposé,* and *doomsday.*

Expository pieces explain their subjects in detail, without extensive controversy or criticism. The conversion of tropical forests to cropland, the role communication plays in our lives, scientific discoveries, manufacturing processes, the functions of government agencies, almost any topic that people are curious about can be given an expository treatment. Like the news story, an expository article answers who, what, where, when, why and how.

Investigative articles focus on the how and why aspects of a subject. They look into an event to find out how and why it happened, or at a certain practice to determine why it exists. They also may expose the pros and cons of such controversial subjects as antidepressants, chemical fertilizers, faith healing, or the use of divining rods to locate water. In order to make the investigative piece work, you must choose a subject open to debate.

Evaluations/reviews examine the attributes of a work of art, performance, place or product, either objectively as in some consumer magazine articles, or subjectively as in the case of book reviews. "How Good is Our Juvenile Justice System," "Rating the Washing Machines," "Do California Wines Measure Up?" and "In Search of the Best Taco in Town" are the sort of titles that tell readers at a glance that the article will give them an evaluation or review of the subject.

Exposés are the "look at how bad it is" pieces. Graft, corruption, cheating, false claims, fraud and public hazards are all grist for the exposé writer's mill. The savings and loan scandal, mismanagement of public funds (such as occurred in the department of Housing and Urban Development), and various environmental abuses are among the more obvious subjects that exposé writers tell us about.

Popular among the exposés are the tabloid articles that reveal all sorts of "information" about celebrities, everything from "secret" diseases they are battling to previous relationships they've hidden from the world.

Doomsday articles are the exposé's first cousins. As times become more threatening, demand for these pieces grows. Instead of exposing a questionable practice or situation, they call attention to some deplorable facet of contemporary society—recession, inflation, pollution, the greenhouse effect, nuclear annihilation—that readers fear. The doomsday pieces, after explaining the dangers to a terrifying point, then usually offer measures the readers can take in order to avoid disaster or protect themselves.

Follow the Leaders

It's not only important to concentrate on the types of articles that sell best. You'll also boost your acceptance ratio by developing articles on the day's—or year's, or decade's—hottest subjects. The following are topics that exploded in popularity during the last years of the 1980s and show no signs of going out of favor: Health and Fitness, Travel, Sports and Outdoors, Business, Computers and Food.

But just any old article about travel or business or food won't do. You must analyze your intended publications to determine which kinds of travel or business or food articles they print.

Health and Fitness

Take *health and fitness*, for example. Within this category, you'll find articles on disease. Pieces may deal with prevention. They may focus on warning symptoms or on treatment. The articles are usually informational, written in the third person, but first and third person accounts of how an individual coped with a disease are also popular. Third-person informational articles often include case histories to illustrate various points.

Articles focusing on mental/emotional health appear in the same forms as those on disease. Women's magazines, especially, feature pieces with titles like "How to Cope Emotionally When Your Man Walks Out" and "How to Beat the Winter Blahs."

You'll notice that these kinds of health articles are written by an expert, by an expert in conjunction with a writer, or by the writer alone. In the last case, however, quotes and information from experts is almost always included.

Nutrition figures heavily in the health and fitness scheme, and you'll find in your analysis that most of the pieces written about eating healthfully are also written by staff members or experts in the field. Be that as it may, there is also room here for the freelancer. Roundup articles telling about celebrities' views on good nutrition, pieces with advice from leading nutritionists, and articles about nutritional breakthroughs all have a good chance of seeing publication if they're well written and targeted at the right publication.

Fitness articles run the gamut from exercise routines to equipment reviews. Largely written by staffers or contributing editors with expertise, they're found in magazines that cater to teens, young singles, businessmen, homemakers, senior citizens, and everyone in between. The niche freelancers find most often is that of reporting on new (or newly revived) forms of exercise. These articles are largely how-tos.

Travel

Over the past decades, there has been an increasing emphasis on quality use of leisure time — couch potatoes notwithstanding. The proliferation of magazines dedicated to travel is good news. The bad news is that every writer seems to like to write about those subjects, so the competition is as stiff as any you'll find.

You'll get a leg up on (or, perhaps more appropriately, a foot ahead of) that competition if you can identify the most salable types of travel and leisure articles.

As far as travel articles are concerned, editors' favorites are:

The broad brush piece, which tells about many of an area's attractions. It's a once-over-lightly piece, devoting a phrase, a sentence, or at most a paragraph to each of the points of interest.

Titles such as "Chicago's Many Faces," "The Cotswolds: England's Captivating Countryside" and "Scandinavia" alert the reader to expect broad brush treatment of the theme.

The place/event piece describes one specific tourist attraction or event in depth, be it an art gallery, posh resort or rock concert. Topics can include everything from projects such as the Truckee River beautification in Reno to Manhattan's Metropolitan Museum of Art to the Prune Festival in Yuba City, California. Before deciding to write this kind of article you must be sure that it's interesting enough to justify a piece of the required word length and that there's sufficient information to write about.

Roundups contain information about several events or

places with a common theme: folk festivals, unusual museums, holiday celebrations and the like. Many roundups include service information such as dates, hours and locations. "Festivals on Ice," "Spa Vacations" and "Centennial Celebrations" are the kinds of titles that identify roundup articles at a glance.

The service article, whether broad brush, roundup or place/event, is set apart by its emphasis on costs, street addresses, and sources of further information. How-to pieces can cover every aspect of travel from taking good pictures through grimy train windows to traveling with your mother-in-law. Budget travel how-tos can be easy sellers during hard times.

The you-are-there articles, heavily laced with anecdotes, quotes and human interest, are intended to give the armchair traveler the feeling of participation. A variation, the first person account, has become increasingly popular during the past few years.

Other travel article best sellers are photo-essays, hard news (especially in travel trade publications) and specialty travel — highlighting such subjects as staying at pousadas in Portugal or snorkeling the Great Barrier Reef.

Where do you look for travel article markets? The most obvious are the magazines devoted exclusively to travel, such as *Travel & Leisure*, *Islands*, *Condé Nast Traveler*, *European Travel & Life*. Inexperienced writers who try to crack these markets, unfortunately, will be almost sure to fail since their material is almost always written by the most skilled writers, writers who have been in the business for years.

Not so well-known travel magazines such as *Caribbean Travel and Life*, *Michigan Living* and *Vista USA* offer greater chances for success.

Although airline in-flights used to be a good place to pitch your pieces, the majority of them currently print only one or two destination pieces per issue, and some don't use any travel at all.

Food and drink publications — notably *Bon Appétit* and *Gourmet*, whose primary emphasis is on food — are good markets for a limited number of experienced writers. Their travel pieces, with titles like "Scenic Swiss Wine Country" (with the subhead "Tasting Cheeses, Chocolates and Chardonnays") generally incorporate the points of interest in an area along with material on regional foods and beverages.

I've found the magazines in this group to be deceptive in that much of the material appears to be the work of freelancers. In actuality, most of it is staff-written or assigned to writers who specialize in food/travel pieces.

Newspaper travel sections and weekly supplements are the biggest market for travel material in the country, and the easiest way for beginning writers to break into print. The major newspapers are listed in *Writer's Market*, but all over the country, smaller dailies and weeklies are on the lookout for articles on interesting places.

The publications in the catchall category of specialized magazines appeal to groups of people with highly divergent interests, philosophies, lifestyles, ages and backgrounds. Travel articles relate directly to the particular magazine's focus, such as pieces on traveling with children in *Working Mother*.

Other kinds of publications that use travel include men's magazines, women's magazines, motor club magazines and magazines published by auto manufacturers, regional magazines, recreational vehicle publications, and house and garden magazines.

Sports and Outdoors

A decade ago, when someone mentioned sports and outdoor magazines, images of football players, golfers, skiers, hunters and fishermen came to mind. Now, if you're an astute analyst, you should see mental pictures of backpackers, rollerbladers, skydivers, snowmobilers, balloonists, snorkelers and all sorts of other people as well.

The 1980s' emphasis on fitness and the out-of-doors left us with an exercise habit. But we like that exercise to be fun. So we don our golf visors and warmups and leotards to pursue the sports and outdoor activities of our choice. And to make our exercise more enjoyable, we want to read about new techniques and equipment, about the experts, about new peaks to conquer.

It's no wonder, then, that editors of the sports/outdoors magazines all select the same basic kinds of articles. They are:

Technique Improvement. Authored by either an expert or the writer in conjunction with an expert, this is a how-to piece —

usually heavily illustrated—that shows the fisherman how to cast farther; the skier how to master moguls; the bowler how to hold the ball so she will get more strikes.

New Product. Since almost every sport or outdoor activity requires equipment—hiking boots, bows and arrows, rackets, ski wax—reviews of new items play a major part in the magazines devoted to these sports and activities. The reviews can be either objective or subjective, depending upon which publication they're written for.

Technical. These are how-to pieces dealing with repair, restoration, building, use and maintenance of equipment such as yachts, ice fishing houses, guns or surfboards.

Profile or Interview. Whatever the sport, it's bound to have heroes—or at least participants who are known for their proficiency. Readers want to know all about these stars: how they got started, how they train, what their goals are, any insights they have into their chosen sport, what they do when they're not practicing and playing/performing.

Place Pieces. These articles tell about specific sites as they relate to the outdoor activity or sport: fishing for muskie on Minnesota's Leech Lake; golfing at St. Andrews in Scotland; roller-blading along the promenade in Venice, California.

Personal Experience. You'll find these most often in the hunting and fishing magazines, where they take the form of first-person accounts of adventures such as tracking wolves or catching marlin with the lightest line possible. You'll occasionally find the personal experience piece in sports magazines, too—accounts of a fifty-year-old executive going to baseball training camp; of a martial arts practitioner who's attacked by a mugger; of a scuba diver's first experience diving off the Great Barrier Reef.

Historical/Nostalgic. Some sports haven't been around long enough to have acquired a history, so you'll only find these pieces in publications devoted to such established sports as baseball, kung fu, tennis and the like.

Business

I'll never confess it to business publication editors, but I almost flunked Econ II in college. To this day I'd have trouble telling you exactly how the Federal Reserve System operates. But that doesn't stop me from writing business articles.

There is such a spread in the degree of expertise required, and so great a variety of magazines to write business pieces for, that the writer can fit herself into any of several niches in the market compatible with her abilities.

Analysis indicates that the following are some best-selling ways to package your ideas when you're writing a business piece:

How He/She/They Did It. One of the easiest for the non-business-oriented writer to analyze and write, this is the kind of article most in demand by trade publications. It shows how a woman who won a blue ribbon for her pickles at the state fair parlayed her pickle-making prowess into a nationally distributed specialty food business, or how a tooling shop proprietor devised a diving board that's used at the Olympics from a discarded airplane wing panel.

The *Business How-to* is almost as easy to put together. How to Maximize Space with Minidisplays, How to Increase Sales with Indirect Lighting, How to Attract Customers in an Offbeat Location—the list is as long as the business writer's imagination. These pieces can be step-by-step or tell how a specific business (or group of businesses) achieved certain results.

Profiles of the man who mass produces gourmet chocolate chip cookies, of the woman who took over her family's failing shoe factory and made it succeed, or of the designer who has created a fortune by disregarding fashion trends aren't only easy to write. They're hot, as far as salability is concerned. Another plus: There are markets for profiles in more magazines than there are for any other kind of business article.

Hard News for national publications is usually taken care of by stringers. These are freelancers who live in various parts of the country and send items from their territories to the editorial offices. Stringing is an excellent way for writers with only a few published pieces to get additional experience, and such a connection isn't too hard to make. All you need to do is to send a battery of letters stating your qualifications to trade journals you would like to write for. Then, if the editor needs someone in your area and your credentials meet with approval, the submission of copy by the deadline and in the publication's style should keep you on the payroll. This doesn't mean that a nonstringer's news submission will never be bought, but you do run the risk that a person has already been assigned to report your area's news.

New Product/New Concept pieces tell about innovations in business and finance. They contain information on everything from new packaging materials to unusual mortgage terms. The degree of technicality in these articles depends upon the perceived level of sophistication of the publication's readership. For example, an article on 1990s applications of Keynesian economics in the *Harvard Business Review* will be much more involved than a piece on new wrinkles in home mortgaging printed in *Family Circle.*

Business Exposé. As consumer advocacy and awareness continue to increase, so does the number of articles highlighting dishonesty and fraud in the business world. Unless you're positive of your facts (and either you or the magazine staff check with an attorney before publication), writing business exposés can be risky business.

The obvious place to sell business articles is to business magazines. Right?

Wrong.

Business writers—people who have specialized in that kind of writing for years—are usually the darlings of the business publication editors as far as their major features are concerned.

Unless you intend to concentrate on business writing and already have some business articles to your credit, you'll spend your marketing time more wisely if you concentrate on trade journals, airline in-flights, and magazines that aren't necessarily read by business people. It usually will be far easier to sell pieces on local businesses to regional magazines, for example, than it will be to sell articles on almost any subject to business publications with national circulation.

The number of nonbusiness publications that use business articles is encouraging. In addition to the in-flights and regionals, women's and men's magazines, general interest publications and travel magazines all print them now and then. Just take a look through any random group of ten or so publications and you'll see that writing business articles is a paying proposition.

Computers

Who would have thought fifteen years ago that computers would be one of the big article topics today? Not everyone, however, can write the articles computer magazine editors would like to buy. This makes explaining computer-related subjects a lucrative field for writers who are computer literate.

There's already a great deal of specialization in the computer magazine arena. In your analysis, you'll find the majority of magazines are for the users of personal computers. These, in turn, are broken down into two groups: magazines for personal computer users regardless of the brand they operate and magazines for users of specific brands such as Atari, IBM and Macintosh.

Other computer magazines focus on microcomputers for handicapped readers, special education and rehabilitation professionals; for programmers; for people shopping for a computer; for people interested in desktop publishing; and for people who make their livelihoods working with computers.

Generally, the kinds of articles you'll find most often in any of these publications are:

Product Reviews. These are reports on new hardware as well as software that point out both strengths and weaknesses. Usually, the reviewed product is compared to others that are similar.

Technical Articles. The province of people who really know their computers, these pieces often contain computer programs devised by their authors.

Interviews/Profiles. CEOs, inventors, well-known computer programmers, and computer game originators are likely subjects for these pieces.

How-tos. Almost all of these tell writers how to write programs or to use software.

Hints and tips, personal experience, tutorials (telling how to use various programs) *and games* are other material that freelancers who are knowledgeable can sell to these publications.

Computer magazines aren't the only markets for articles about computers. Pick up almost any airline in-flight, any business magazine or publication read by people in business and you're apt to find articles about these electronic marvels that will play an increasingly important role in our lives.

Generally, these articles aren't as complex as those in the computer magazines and are the easiest for most freelancers to write. If you can write an article simplifying anything having to do with computers, chances are you'll find buyers for your pieces. And if you have the talent for sounding funny on paper, humorous computer pieces ought to sell faster than PCs.

Food

Food, from the late 1970s through the 1980s, was transformed from just something to eat to an art form. Yuppies considered preparing food on weekends a sort of recreational, leisure time activity. The fast-food backlash also contributed to the popularity of magazine articles on food and its preparation. And now that people have discovered that it is fun to read about food, these articles are sure to stay popular for a while.

The principal types of food features are roundups of recipes — "Ten Chocolate Cakes," "Autumn Harvest Soups," "S-u-m-m-e-r Spells Ice Cream" — that are usually written by staffers; articles about certain kinds of food such as mushrooms or apples; and pieces featuring the entertainment style of a particular person, couple or family.

Add these to the articles on nutrition and food-focused travel mentioned above, as well as restaurant reviews, and you'll see that there's an expanding market for writers who like to eat and to write about it.

I've written about food in a variety of ways: on recipe contesting for *Woman's Day*; about oysters for Delta Airline's *Sky*; about foods produced and manufactured in Nevada, the state's candymakers, Nevada's ethnic foods, and special holiday dishes Nevada casino chefs prepare, all for *Nevada Magazine*. As you can see, the range of subject matter is pretty diverse, as are the publications. I have yet to write a humorous piece about food, but am convinced by the few funny food pieces I *have* seen that those pieces are in demand.

Markets for food-focused articles include — in addition to the food and drink publications — house and garden magazines, some airline in-flights, regional magazines, women's publications, general interest magazines, travel and recreational vehicle magazines, and specialty magazines galore.

Analysis is vital if you want to sell articles featuring food, as each magazine has its own tastes. Obvious, of course, is the fact that if you want to sell to *Chocolatier*, you must write about something related to chocolate. But requirements are far more subtle when specialized magazines are considered.

By concentrating on the best sellers, you can be assured that your by-line will keep appearing again and again. Because your articles will be best sellers, too.

Chapter Ten

That's the Idea!

> *If you have had your attention directed to the novelties of thought in your own lifetime, you will have observed that almost all really new ideas have a certain aspect of foolishness when they are first produced, and almost any idea which jogs you out of your current abstractions may be better than nothing.*
>
> Alfred North Whitehead, *Adventures of Ideas*

Of all the definitions of the word *idea*—and you'll find more than a half dozen definitions in most dictionaries—the one that suits the writer's needs best is "a design; a preliminary plan; often, a plan or purpose of action."

It is the most suitable because, for the successful writer, a salable idea is not only a concept. It also involves refining that concept, shaping it, slanting it, giving it focus. The initial idea is often only the launching pad that modifications take off from. And it may be the fifth, or sixth or seventh generation of the original concept that finally becomes the nucleus of an article.

In short, when we say salable idea, we're not talking about

"good" ideas. We are talking about the right idea for a particular publication—the idea that our analysis shows us will be on the mark in its subject, treatment, breadth of focus, slant. Coming up with salable ideas requires, first of all, a clear notion of the kinds of magazines you would like to write for, magazines whose content dovetails with your areas of interest and expertise.

Becoming familiar with a large variety of publications is the basic way of deciding which ones will offer you the greatest chance of success. But there are additional methods you can use to zero in on your target magazines.

The following is an excellent device for deciding what kinds of magazines you should write for while coming up with basic ideas at the same time.

Take several 8½ × 11-inch sheets of paper. At the top of each of them write headings such as:

1. Jobs I've Held
2. Places I've Lived
3. My Skills
4. My Hobbies
5. Interesting/Inspirational People I've Met
6. Interesting/Inspirational Co-workers
7. Interesting/Inspirational Friends and Neighbors
8. Places I've Traveled
9. Projects I've Made/Built
10. Problems I've Dealt With/Overcome
11. Sports I Participate In
12. Unusual Experiences/Relationships I've Had

You will come up with other headings as well. For example, big-name entertainers perform year-round at the casinos in my city, Reno, and nearby Lake Tahoe. I might, therefore, look over the casinos' schedules of upcoming attractions and make a list of celebrities who would possibly be available for interviews.

Perhaps you're the owner of a small business. You might want to make several lists nonbusiness owners could never come up with—"Hidden Costs of Doing Business," "Special Sales Techniques," "Labor-Saving Methods" and the like.

As an operating room nurse, some of your headings may well be the same as those of a coffee distributor; others will be markedly different. If you're an architect, a baker, a recreation professional, your occupation in itself will lend itself to subject headings not common to the rest of us.

But whatever your headings, you should next start making lists under them, leaving plenty of white space between each place or project or experience you write down. This list-making should be an ongoing process. Don't try to do it all in one sitting, since once you get started, additions to the list are likely to keep popping up during your everyday tasks and, sometimes, in the middle of the night.

In the course of your list-making, you'll realize more clearly where your interests lie. If each time you make an addition to a certain list, for example, there's not even a flicker of interest, you pretty well can be assured that writing about the subject would be sheer drudgery and would result in a dull piece.

If, on the other hand, the additions to another subject heading give you an "it would be so much fun to write about that" feeling, chances are you've found an area that should be pursued.

While you're in your list-making mode, you will automatically notice magazines that contain articles about subjects like those you've written down. The ski magazine you subscribe to frequently runs articles on cost-cutting; how about one featuring advice on organizing a kid's ski swap, a subject you added to your list only yesterday? And this month's issue of your state's official magazine had a profile of a pioneer baker, which makes you wonder if they would like one about the early-day candymaker on your list.

After you've made a number of entries on each page and discarded—at least temporarily—those pages that haven't evoked enough interest, start expanding each entry with additional information. Under "Co-workers," tell why they are interesting or inspirational. List anything that sets places where you have lived apart from others. Amplify your hobbies with techniques you have devised to make them easier, variations that make them different.

As you can see, these sheets of paper become working blueprints you can use throughout your career as a writer. The lists can be expanded and amended through the years, and will serve as a never-ending source of ideas.

As you continue to prime the idea pump, you'll find that the germinal thoughts flow faster and faster. You'll get ideas from speakers, seminars and panel discussions. Asking experts will give you ideas on everything from microbiology to managing a produce department. Attending symposia on science and health, reading newspapers and magazines, eavesdropping on conversations at the drugstore will add to your supply of potential subjects to write about.

Sometimes you'll get ideas by broadening a local story idea to give it national appeal or by localizing or personalizing a national story. Perhaps you live in Yuba City, California, and each September read about the annual Prune Festival. Or perhaps your local newspaper carries a story about a community program to combat animal abuse.

If you're a writer who enjoys eating, the first article may prompt you to begin keeping a file of festivals centered around food that are held throughout the country each year. Animal activist/writers will possibly have easy access to information on anti-abuse campaigns in other parts of the nation.

Localizing or personalizing a national story is even easier. Although you may not find as many markets for this kind of article, it often works for regional publications. "Scams that Rob the Poor" in a national publication might lead you to do some investigative reporting on the subject as it pertains to your area. A national article on immigration might be narrowed to one about the ethnic composition of immigrants to your part of the country.

The most salable ideas often come from our own experiences. Being fired from a job, starting a new career, having to care for aging parents or to deal with recalcitrant teenagers puts us on the front line — right out there with thousands of our fellow men.

If, like one of my former students, we suspect that a parking lot accident was deliberately staged by the other party, we have an article idea along with the dented fender. When a doctor charges us eighty dollars for a five-minute look at our ear and a phone call to a specialist, we start thinking about a potential piece on surviving without health insurance as we write out the check.

Two days later—and this sort of thing happens a lot more often than you would imagine—we hear in casual conversation about a friend who also had a fender-bender that she suspects happened accidentally on purpose. No sooner have we jotted down her name and phone number on the appropriate sheet than we read some statistics: thirty-seven million Americans have no health insurance; 28 percent of the population either is under-insured or has no health insurance; even with Medicare, older Americans are forced to spend more than 15 percent of their income annually for medical care.

This process is a continuing one. But having sheets full of fleshed-out ideas and some thoughts about where we might market them is not enough. Our next task is to select the winners. Or most likely, to take our most promising ideas and, in the context of the magazines we see them fitting into, refine those ideas into the concepts that have the best chances of eliciting editor approval.

After pairing up article idea and potential publication—but before writing that all-important query letter—it's time to picture the reader. Remember, that's who the editor wants to please. Will you target your nonaccidental accident idea for an insurance agent's journal? For an RV magazine? A publication that's aimed at sports car drivers?

By using the tools we've discussed in previous chapters to gather clues about the publication's readership and coupling it with your own mental images based on insurance agents, RVers, or sports car drivers you've known, you will be able to select the sorts of information appropriate to your intended magazine. Then, after taking into consideration such elements as point of view, style, and tone of the magazine, you'll be ready to write your query.

Time was when that query would work almost as well with Magazine A as with Magazine Z. In fact, many writers still revise or print out fresh copies of rejected queries and send them off to other editors without changing a word (except the address). That's a crucial mistake in this era of specialization.

Let's look at the retirement publications as an example, since they are and promise to continue to be among the fastest growing group of publications. In point of fact, we really shouldn't even lump them all as "Retirement Publications" or "Publications for Seniors" as their readership, formats and styles are so diverse. The dozen publication profiles below include less than half of those aimed at the fiftysomething-and-over crowd:

Active American. The focus is on exercise, nutrition and health. Photos show older, obviously healthy adults biking, roller-blading, swimming, working out with weights. The articles all have a positive slant, including information that readers can use to make their own lives more healthful. Recipes and nutritional articles are directed at reducing calories, cholesterol, and other substances currently believed to be bad for us.

Golden Years. With one of the broadest menus of subject matter, topics covered range from old-time diners and thatched roofs to money management and cardiac catheterization. An article on grandparents raising grand and great-grandchildren, a profile on radio personality Larry King, and travel pieces on San Francisco, Chicago and Dallas helped round out the eclectic offerings of a single issue.

Mature Traveler. This tabloid-style publication is completely devoted to travel from the perspective of the forty-nine-and-over generation. Each issue contains one major destination piece, usually written in first person by a freelancer.

Mature Living. Published monthly by the Sunday School Board of the Southern Baptist Convention, this magazine has a definite religious orientation and is designed for "senior adults sixty and older." Subject matter is heavy on nostalgia with a method—"My Father Never Said 'I Love You'," "The Old Porch Swing," "I Remember Melons, Wagons, and Summertime"—but also runs service articles such as "Beware of Unidentified Service People." The writing is less sophisticated than in most of the senior publications.

Mature Outlook. Sponsored by the Mature Outlook Association, "a member of the Sears family of companies," the magazine is published by Meredith Publishing Corporation, which also puts out *Better Homes and Gardens* and *Grandparents* magazine. It's no surprise, therefore, to find the editorial mix of health, leisure time and travel activities augmented by *Better Homes and Gardens* type pieces on gardening and home decoration.

Mature Years. Material in this magazine is the most religiously oriented of any of the publications profiled here. Although there are articles about subjects such as white water rafting and skills people have learned in their later years, the majority of the pages are devoted to devotions and to articles with a spiritual message.

Modern Maturity. Best known of the publications for seniors, this is the most difficult for beginning writers to break into. Content is wide ranging, from the meaning of dreams to how to subcontract your home-building project. Since the magazine goes to members of the American Association of Retired Persons (AARP), which has a membership of thirty million, this is one of the largest circulation magazines in the country.

New Choices for the Best Years. This magazine is younger in outlook than the other leading senior publications. Many of its readers are still working full time, and the others are portrayed as being vital, active, younger than their years. Subject matter is eclectic, and without the photos, the magazine is more like non-age-targeted general interest publications than its competitors.

Prime Times. Another of the younger outlook publications for seniors, this is a topical magazine of broad general appeal. Investigative reporting, profiles, and fiction as well as consumer issues and life-style planning are the result of the magazine's editorial slant—redefining mid-life and retirement life-style and promoting a dynamic vision of the young prime-life years.

Senior Edition USA. This is an example of a regional tabloid directed at seniors. Published in Denver, it combines national news and features of interest to its age-group readers as well as items of interest to and articles written by Colorado residents.

Senior Life. A Southern California publication, this one reminds me of something my grandmother would have liked to read. Though the tag line says it's "The Magazine for Active Adults," the articles all have a homeyness about them—memories of the golden days of radio, recalling tennis in the "Good Ole Days," slightly new twists on recipes for comfort food, craft projects.

Senior World. "Serving active older adults of San Diego County" is the tag line on this regional tabloid. It's more like a newspaper in both content and style than any of the other publications profiled here. There are pages devoted to Travel,

Home, Health and Living sections along with the hard news, ads and classifieds.

Now that we've taken a look at some of these publications, let's get down to cases by taking an idea from generation to the senior magazine market.

Say you're fiftysomething yourself and love to travel. Since you always take lots of notes, you have pages written about various trips and aspects of travel after only a couple of sessions with your idea lists.

Realizing that you could go on making lists forever, you decide to start refining the ideas you've put down and selecting a couple of them for possible articles. You decide that you would like to write for the senior market, so your next job is to assemble all your back copies of those publications you have that print travel articles.

You have also decided that rate of pay doesn't matter as much as publication, so the array of magazines is larger than it would have been had you felt, for instance, that it wasn't worth your time to write for less than ten cents a word.

In your pile are eight of the publications profiled above: *Golden Years*, *Mature Outlook*, *Mature Traveler*, *Mature Years*, *Modern Maturity*, *New Choices*, *Prime Times*, and *Senior World*. You eliminate two of them within a few minutes. You see that virtually all of the travel articles in *Modern Maturity* are written by the travel editor. *Mature Outlook*'s travel editor also appears to put together most, if not all, of that magazine's articles about destinations.

After reading the travel articles in the four remaining magazines, you go back to your list. Two of your ideas — or variations thereof — seem promising. You at first had in mind a broad brush piece about Finland. But lots of people would be apt to submit pieces of that sort, you reckon. So, since *New Choices* often uses three articles on similar subjects such as "Let's Make Tracks" (blurbed as three great vacations by train) and "Great Short Stops" (three spectacular weekend trips), you just know that sometime they'll want to do boat trips. Your trip through the Finnish lake country might be just what the editor is looking for and would have a better chance than the broad brush piece.

Your second idea involves a recent elderhostel experience

in Asia. The diary you kept on that trip is full of anecdotes and things said by various people you met along the way, but you also have reams of hard facts. Lists of prices for things you purchased, train fares and the like.

Mature Traveler's first person accounts, you notice, are augmented by sidebars. The format is perfect for your material. You are ready to send out queries to two magazines and have ideas galore left to work with while you're waiting for the editors' responses.

But perhaps you're not ready to write for the senior publications yet, so let's work with another idea. Under your list that's headed "Hobbies," you write "Skiing." After making some notes about ski resorts where you have stayed, mountains you have skied, equipment you've liked, or problems you have encountered, you decide that "Skiing" deserves a separate sheet of its own.

At some time in this process, you gather together the current year's issues of skiing magazines you like best. You have a stack of four publications: *Ski, Skiing, Snow Country* and *Powder*.

You notice that *Snow Country* (with the tag line "The Year-Round Magazine of Mountain Sports and Living") almost always carries at least one article on the sorts of places one stays when skiing, be they rentals or friends' places or second homes.

On your "Skiing" sheet, you have a number of scribbles about the chalet you and a couple who were (but didn't remain) your best friends built from a manufactured housing kit.

That article idea won't fit, you realize, because all the mountain dwelling articles are about satisfactory arrangements. Furthermore, they tell about arrangements that have survived through the years, that people are happy with.

Next, you recall a co-worker who, with three other single parents, bought a weekend mountain retreat. You remember that during that winter, her conversation consisted of a litany of the disasters associated with co-op ownership. The next season, after the quartet had worked together to solve their problems, she couldn't stop talking about the joys of sharing a vacation place.

You're about to discard that idea for the same reasons you rejected its predecessor. Then you realize that *Snow Country* not only uses articles on winter homes, the editor is also big on how-tos — "Turn Kids on to Skiing," "Get Started in Snowboarding," "Look Behind the Agent's Door" (advice about rental agencies).

The editor, you realize, could very possibly go for a piece on ground rules for co-op vacation retreats. You have a number of ideas on what soured your construction project. Your co-worker can tell you why their co-op venture almost failed and what the participants did to make it work. You will be able to obtain advice from counselors, mediators and the like to give readers their expert opinions.

You'll notice that *Snow Country*'s how-to articles often include sidebars, such as "Seven Steps to a Higher Occupancy Rate," which accompanied the rental agent piece. That tells you that readers want hard facts in addition to personal experiences.

You'll also note that despite the fact that the magazine carries a number of articles about upscale resorts and equipment (after all, skiing is an expensive sport), there's emphasis on affordability in the vacation home pieces. Because skiing is expensive, it may be that readers sacrifice in other ways in order to have good equipment and a four-wheel-drive vehicle that will get them to the slopes.

And don't ignore the fact that although most of the people pictured in the magazine are in the twenty to forty age group, others are over fifty. Slant your article to a readership that includes the veteran of real estate transactions as well as the first-time property owner.

As you can see, you've come a long way from the vague references to Finland and elderhostel you first put on your list, from the "Hobbies" heading to "Rules for Vacation Co-op Coexistence," but the time you put into matchmaking idea and publication will save you time and rejection in the long run.

Chapter Eleven

Now It's Up to You

> *If you define your future by what you are doing today, you will be in big trouble.*
>
> Christopher Hegarty, *USAir*, June, 1990

*F*or most people who like to write, dilemma time comes not long after they embark on their writing careers. That's because we writers are a curious breed. We want to know almost everything about almost everything. We're at the library researching 1950s music and have to fight being seduced by 1930s collectibles, 1940s slang, 1960s protests, and all the other fascinating topics we encounter along the way. At an interview for a piece about raising oysters in man-made beds, the interviewee mentions shrimp farming and another article idea pops unbidden into our cranial file. But we simply can't write about *everything*.

Fortunately, there are a few subjects that leave us glassy-eyed. But there are many more that start our mental motors running. So we have to make choices. In many cases, our economic survival as freelancers depends on them. In others, it's a matter of psychic gratification.

First, you must ask yourself if you want to build expert status by specializing in certain types of subjects, writing for specific publications. Although when I began freelancing, I wrote about anything and everything editors would pay me for, the time came seven or eight years later when I decided to concentrate on travel writing.

Since that's the field I know best, let's use it by way of illustration. Say the idea of being a travel writer appeals to you, too. Before you decide to devote your writing time to telling about places and pleasures, you'll want to analyze the costs versus the rewards.

It's a good idea to talk, if you can, to established writers in the field. Ask them about how much money successful travel writers can reasonably expect to make (usually quite a bit less than business or technical writers). Seek their honest assessment of how tough the competition can be (very). Inquire about the lifestyle (an extremely enjoyable one if you're able to produce enough salable copy that magazines will pay your expenses or tourism officials regularly invite you to visit their cities and/or countries).

In your enthusiasm don't forget to ask about the disadvantages and the sort of personality you'll need to succeed. The travel writer must, for example, be extremely flexible: Be able to fly halfway around the world on two day's notice if an economically feasible opportunity presents itself; stay a week longer than planned at a destination if it's necessary to the story; sleep all night sitting up on trains; get up at six in the morning and go to bed at midnight in order to cram the maximum into every day; accept strange foods and different cultures without freaking out; report about people, places and customs without becoming judgmental.

As with travel writing, each kind of specialization has different requirements. Although all writers should strive for accuracy, business writers must be sticklers. People who write about people need to be especially easy to talk to and non-threatening. Food writers have to be eclectic in their tastes, be open to new ideas, know their way around the kitchen/market, and be prepared for the rare case of food poisoning (it truly does happen).

From Specialist to Expert . . . or Generalist?

After you have decided to concentrate on one area of writing, you'll often have to make more decisions in order to gain your expert status. Travel writers usually specialize in certain areas of the world (Europe, the Caribbean, the Pacific Rim); kinds of travel (budget, luxury, single, family); and/or modes of transport, such as RV or cruise ship. They may work to be known by travel editors as "the travel writer in Colorado who specializes in ski resorts" or the "man in San Francisco who writes about train travel."

Health and fitness writers may choose to become known as authorities on such subjects as nutrition, new forms of exercise, spas or bioethics. They may concentrate their writing on relationships that result from divorce, on eating disorders, or on cosmetic surgery.

Most writers—especially at the beginning of their careers—choose to be generalists. The advantages to this approach are easy to see. You get to test the waters, exploring a variety of subjects and writing styles. You never get bored since each article is usually vastly different from the last.

The disadvantages are not so obvious. As a generalist, you'll rarely get a phone call from an editor assigning you a specific kind of article. Writing for a number of publications will mean that it takes longer for you to sell a number of pieces to each of them. As a result, you won't be able to command the rates at the higher end of their payment schedule that are generally reserved for frequent contributors. The difference between being a regular contributor and an occasional one at the medium-paying publications can mean three hundred to a thousand dollars and more an article.

The Market-Go-Round

Whether you decide to be a specialist or a generalist, you must become committed to keeping abreast with both the markets and the times in order to succeed. While the premise of this book is that the analytical freelancer can determine what an editor will buy in the future by studying what she has bought in the past, we must keep in mind that magazines do not exist in a vacuum. What the editor will buy must also be put in the context of what is going on in the world around it.

It's like a fascinating game, with multiple sets of changing rules. The multitude of interdependent variables that make up society keeps magazines — the reflectors of that society's values, concerns, pleasures and goals — accommodating the interests of their readers within their respective formats.

As our life-styles change, so do the publications that are launched to complement them. Every successful freelancer constantly checks out the markets, being on the lookout for the new publications, keeping track of those that have folded.

And the changes in a magazine's purpose, outlook and format can be enormous, if you analyze it over a span of years. *Gourmet*, as you may or may not recall, started out in 1941 as a magazine for male food hobbyists.

United Airline's in-flight magazine, called *Mainliner* a decade ago, has been renamed *Vis a Vis* and bears little resemblance to the former publication. Now a series of short takes on everything from rare art to upscale picnic baskets rarely more than a page in length, it mirrors the fast-track, I-want-it-all life-style of the 1980s. Since the 1990s philosophy is quite different, we can expect to see corresponding changes in the philosophies of United's magazine, and others as well.

The astute freelancer always keeps in mind factors like the state of the economy, the political climate, whether the country is on the brink of war. He analyzes current trends, consumption habits, states of mind. For example, during energy crunches, the successful travel writer concentrates on close-to-home destinations rather than cross-country or across-the-globe trips.

We all have seen enough kinds of life-styles go in and out of vogue to realize that we must adjust our article angles to those that are currently considered desirable or interesting to read about. We know that an article emphasizing the necessity of a business having a big entertainment budget won't find many takers when the country is plunged in a recession; that a piece on making the client feel like a king without bearing him gifts will. We realize that when most people are in an ecological state of mind, they won't care to read articles that condone frivolous use of our natural resources.

Changes in mores and levels of machismo are reflected in magazines for men and women. The shift toward marriage during the late 1980s was reflected by articles such as "How to Close the Deal (Get Married)" in *Cosmo* and "Men & Marriage—What They Want, Why They Wait" in *Glamour*. At the same time, men's magazines started placing more emphasis on sultry TV actresses, "investigative reports" on whether bikinis are getting too small, "blood" sports and other topics that we're told appeal to "real men."

If the paragraphs above sound extreme and you need to be convinced of natural evolution in magazines, go to the library some rainy afternoon and browse through a stack of magazines published ten or twenty years ago. Not only will you be impressed with how much better photos and layout are than they were in those days, you'll be amazed to see that several of the kinds of articles editors bought then—both as far as style and content are concerned—wouldn't have a chance of acceptance at most publications today.

I rely primarily on the sources we discussed in chapter one to find out about new magazines. Information in *Publishers Weekly*, *Advertising Age*, the *Wall Street Journal* and *Writer's Digest* helps me learn about magazines that have gone out of business. It's important not only to find out which magazines have ceased publication. The analytical writer also discovers why.

Several paragraphs down in the *Wall Street Journal* article "Fame Magazine Halts Publication After Two Years" was some information I've tucked away in the marketing compartment of my brain (I've also put the clipping in my files as back-up). Here's what I found most informative in this article, which had begun by saying the magazine was shutting its doors because its founder and publisher, Steven Greenberg, estimated that advertising pages for the monthly wouldn't grow in 1991 and that he needed to invest heavily to increase the magazine's circulation:

> In a difficult publishing climate, the folding of *Fame* isn't considered a surprise, particularly because it published independently of any other magazine titles. Most of the magazines that have gone out of business in 1990 published independently or were part of small publishing groups . . . .
>
> "We would have had a market in the 1980s, but the '80s are over," Mr. Greenberg said. "In 1991, many magazines are going to look (as thin as) pamphlets."

The "Advertising" column in the *Wall Street Journal*'s second section also yields occasional tips when it talks about advertising revenues at various magazines or tells where advertising agencies are placing their clients' ads.

As a result of keeping up with this kind of trade talk, you put yourself ahead of the competition. You'll find out which kinds of magazines are struggling to pay the printers (and their writers). You will be among the first to know about emerging trends in publishing. And since you have learned to analyze magazines vis-à-vis their advertisements, you'll have an inside track by knowing what kinds of articles to pitch to the editors of which magazines.

As important as keeping abreast of the state of the industry and the tempo of the times is having a feel for the current fashions in publications generally and your targeted magazines in particular.

For example, magazine style in the next few years promises to be more casual and upbeat than ever before—*Los Angeles Magazine* and *Spy* are good examples of this trend toward a breezy, irreverent style. The reason for this is simple. Each year, the electronic media—with entertaining, easy-to-watch magazine-type features—provide increasing competition.

We must pay attention, too, to which kinds of magazines are becoming less popular and which are gaining larger followings.

The already mentioned trend toward specialty magazines promises to remain strong. But since fads and fancies come and go, concentrating on only one of them as a market is about the most precarious perch a freelancer can light on unless the subject your magazine specializes in is one that's sure to stay around for a while.

Magazines for seniors will undoubtedly remain vital and proliferate. There will undoubtedly be more specialization within the senior market. We have already seen the beginnings of this trend with the emergence of such publications as *Active American*, which deals exclusively with health and fitness for people in their later years, and *Mature Traveler*.

You will sense a real need for increased "understandability" in the computer magazines you have read—or tried to read. It's a good bet that publishers have noticed that need, too, and will set about addressing it as more people buy home computers.

This means that articles lighter in style and less technical will become more salable.

As a group, the regional magazines seem to be getting healthier than they have ever been. Not only is their content becoming more interesting; the quality of paper and layout is improving as advertising revenues and/or sponsoring organization support increases.

Some regionals, of course, are born losers. Every person with money who has "always wanted to publish a magazine" chooses to launch one either about his favorite sport or the area she lives in (or has "always wanted to move to"). These would-be publishers seem unaware of the competition for advertising dollars and, after a few issues, get tired of being eaten alive by expenses. It's all right, of course, to submit to new regionals, but you'll have a better chance of seeing the paychecks if you write for those that are well established.

Regionals will remain one of the easiest groups of magazines for writers to break into. They're especially desirable markets because the writer doesn't have to go far from home for his research. Best of all, you usually don't have to plan megamile trips in order to meet the editors.

Trade publications continue to be the undiscovered markets for freelancers. Even though videocassettes on making sales, production techniques, merchandising and store display are becoming more readily available to businesses and manufacturers, they haven't seemed to have cut into the trades' popularity.

The kinds of magazines mentioned above are only a sampling of the markets freelancers should be thinking about when they're plotting their freelancing futures. By putting your analytical techniques to work, you'll be able to look at any magazine realistically and figure out whether you can fit into its future.

Your analysis should be an ongoing process. My editor and freelance friends are spending a considerable amount of time thinking about the forms magazines will take during the next years and preparing themselves to be ready for the changes to come.

Friendly Exchange editor Adele Malott believes that magazines will become more personalized, that individuals will literally be able to order their own very personalized magazines, consisting of exactly the kinds of articles they want to read. "I don't know exactly how it will work," she says, "but the technology is here now—fax machines, modems and the like—to make it happen."

Minneapolis freelancer Carla Waldemar, who is also food and art editor of the *Twin Cities Reader*, says magazine articles of the future will be "short and snappy. I just see the written word retrenching. I see the magazine becoming an informative source rather than a literary source. The consumer—I use that term rather than 'reader'—doesn't choose to give the time to reading."

The Final Analysis

Whatever the future brings, there will still be a need for writers as information givers, whether it be in the form of database providers or crafters of prose as we know it today. If you use analysis, that future will be brighter for you.

Writing on target is not a skill you'll acquire all at once. It will take time and energy to learn how to effectively analyze the articles you read. But I think you will find the results worth every bit of your effort. There's a definite thrill when an editor tells you, "We like the piece and are planning to use it in our July issue." It's exciting to watch that bank balance grow.

The writer's life is good times and bad times, pleasures mixed with pain. I wouldn't change my career for anything in the world. What I have changed through analysis, however, is the proportion of pleasure, by tipping the acceptance/rejection ratio mightily in my favor. You can do it, too.

Index